GW00455754

CONGESTIVE

HEART FAILURE

Cookbook for Beginners

1200 Days of Healthy and Delicious Low Sodium & Low Fat Recipes to Improve your Heart Health and Reduce Blood Pressure

Julie L. Cook

Copyright© 2023 by Julie L. Cook

All rights reserved worldwide.

No part of this book may be reproduced or transmitted in any form or by any means, electronic or mechanical, including photo- copying, recording or by any information storage and retrieval system, without written permission from the publisher, except for the inclusion of brief quotations in a review.

Warning-Disclaimer

The purpose of this book is to educate and entertain. The author or publisher does not guarantee that anyone following the techniques, suggestions, tips, ideas, or strategies will become successful. The author and publisher shall have neither liability or responsibility to anyone with respect to any loss or damage caused, or alleged to be caused, directly or indirectly by the information contained in this book.

TABLE OF CONTENT

INTRODUCTION

"Nourishing Recipes for Congestive heart failure." This cookbook was designed specifically to assist individuals who suffer from congestive cardiac failure to adopt a delicious and healthy diet that supports cardiovascular health. Congestive Heart Failure is a condition where the heart cannot pump blood effectively, resulting in fluid buildup and possible complications.

It is important to eat well in order to manage congestive cardiac failure. Making healthy food choices can help you maintain a healthy diet and support the heart.

This book aims to provide you with easy-to-follow recipes which prioritize nutrition and flavor. The recipes have been carefully designed to use ingredients low in cholesterol, sodium and saturated fats. Discover a wide range of delicious dishes to suit different tastes, diets, and preferences.

This cookbook offers not only healthy recipes but also valuable tips on how you can modify your cooking methods to be more heart-friendly. There are helpful tips on how to reduce sodium, choose heart-healthy oils, add more fiber and manage portion sizes.

This cookbook does not replace professional medical guidance or dietary advice. Consult your doctor or registered dietitian to tailor diet recommendations for your needs.

You will be able to embark on an exciting culinary journey with "The Heart Healthy Cookbook: Nourishing recipes for Congestive Heart Failure". This book is your guide as you strive towards a happier, healthier life. Discover the delight of heart-healthy, delicious meals that will nourish your body as well as your soul.

Why Is Nutrition Important For Congestive Heart Failure?

The role of nutrition in the management of congestive cardiac failure is crucial, as it has a direct impact on the progress of the condition and the overall health of those with the condition. Congestive heart disease is affected by nutrition.

Fluid Balance: CHF can lead to swelling in the lungs and other parts of the body. By regulating salt (sodium) intake in a heart-healthy way, you can maintain fluid balance and prevent fluid retention. Monitor and reduce sodium intake to control fluid retention and symptoms of CHF.

Blood Pressure Control: CHF can be caused by high levels of blood pressure.

Lowering blood pressure can be achieved by a heart-healthy, low sodium, high fruit, vegetable, and whole grain diet such as DASH. By controlling blood pressure, heart failure progression can be slowed, and the workload for the heart reduced.

Weight Management: It is important to maintain a healthy body weight when managing CHF. Weight gain puts extra strain on the body, which makes it difficult for the heart to pump blood efficiently. Weight management can be achieved by a well-balanced, healthy diet that includes portion control and calories.

Nutrient Intake: Nutritional deficiencies can occur in people with CHF due to a lack of appetite, medication, or restrictions on diet. In order to maintain good health, consuming a diet rich in nutrients is essential. The heart's proper function depends on nutrients such as potassium and magnesium. These are usually depleted by CHF.

Managing Coexisting Conditions: CHF can coexist with conditions like diabetes, high blood pressure, and obesity. A heart-healthy diet will help you manage all of these health conditions. It can reduce the risks and promote overall cardiovascular health.

Energy Levels: CHF may cause fatigue or a reduction in energy. An optimally balanced diet will optimize your energy and promote physical activity. Maintaining energy allows individuals with CHF to engage in daily activities and appropriate exercise, which has a positive effect on their heart health.

For individuals suffering from CHF, it is essential that they work closely with the healthcare team, including nutritionists and registered dietitians, to design a nutrition plan tailored to their needs.

Tips for Shopping For and Meal Planning With Congestive Heart Failure

In order to create a diet and shopping list that is healthy for your heart, it's best to focus on heart-healthy products and create a balance of foods. You can use these tips when shopping and planning meals for CHF.

Consult with a healthcare professional or registered dietitian: Consult a dietitian or healthcare professional before making significant changes in your diet. You can get personalized advice that is based on the specific needs of your health and dietary restrictions.

Limit sodium intake: When you shop for ingredients, choose low-sodium or sodium-free options. When shopping for food, choose low-sodium options or those that are sodium-free. Aim for foods with less sodium than 140mg per portion. Processed and canned food tends to have high sodium levels.

Choose fresh, whole foods: Include fresh vegetables, fruits, grains, proteins and fats in your diet. They are rich in nutrients and help to promote good heart health. Choose colorful fruits and vegetables and select whole grain options like brown rice, whole wheat bread, and quinoa.

Opt for lean proteins: Lean proteins like tofu, beans, salmon (or other fish), trout and tuna, as well as skinless chicken, are great sources of protein. Reduce the intake of red meats as they are higher in saturated fatty acids.

Emphasize heart-healthy fats: Include heart-healthy fats in your diet, like avocados, almonds, seeds and olive oil. These fats may help to reduce inflammation and promote heart health. Use them moderately due to the high caloric content.

Portion control: To prevent weight gain and overeating, pay attention to portion size. You can use measuring cups and food scales to make sure you are eating the right amount of food from every food group. You will be able to maintain healthy calories by doing this.

Meal prep and plan ahead: By planning your meals ahead of time, you can make better choices. You will also avoid unhealthy last-minute options. Plan your weekly meals and create an e-list. Prepare some ingredients ahead of time. For convenience, consider batch cooking your meals and storing them in portions-sized containers.

Cook at home: You can control the cooking method and ingredients better when you prepare your meals yourself. This reduces the consumption of foods that are high in fats and sodium.

Experiment with herbs and spices: Instead of using salt, use herbs, spices and citrus juices to add flavor. It will reduce the sodium in your diet while adding great flavors to all your meals.

Stay hydrated: It is important to maintain heart health by ensuring that you are adequately hydrated. Water, herbal tea or infused waters are better alternatives to sugary drinks.

It's important to collaborate with your medical team in order to develop a customized meal plan to meet your needs.

CHAPTER 1: BREAKFAST RECIPES

Cheese and Vegetable Frittata

Preparation Time: 10 minutes

Cooking Time: 25 minutes

Total Time: 35 minutes

Ingredients

- 6 large eggs
- 1/4 cup of milk
- 1/2 cup of shredded cheddar cheese
- 1/2 cup of diced bell peppers (any color)
- 1/2 cup of diced zucchini
- 1/4 cup of diced red onion
- 1/4 cup of sliced mushrooms
- 2 tbsp chopped fresh parsley
- Salt and pepper as needed
- 1 tbsp olive oil

Instructions

1. Preheat your oven to 375°F.
2. Whisk the eggs, milk, salt, and pepper until well blended in a large bowl.
3. In an oven-safe skillet set over medium heat, warm the olive oil.
4. To the pan, add the diced bell peppers, zucchini, red onion, and mushrooms. Approximately 5

minutes of sautéing is required to gently soften the veggies.

5. Over the skillet's sautéed veggies, pour the egg mixture.
6. Over the eggs and veggies, evenly distribute the shredded cheddar cheese.
7. The frittata should be cooked on the stovetop for 3 to 4 minutes or until the edges begin to firm.
8. Bake the frittata for 15-18 minutes, or until it is set in the center and has a light golden brown top, in the preheated oven.
9. After removing the pan from the oven, give the frittata some time to cool.
10. Add freshly cut parsley as a garnish.
11. Serve the frittata warm, cut into wedges.

Nutritional Information (approximate values per serving)

Calories: 250 Fat: 17g Carbohydrates: 6g Protein: 18g Fiber: 2g

Quinoa with Cinnamon and Peaches

Preparation Time: 5 minutes

Cooking Time: 15-20 minutes

Total Time: 20-25 minutes

Ingredients

- 1 cup of quinoa
- 2 cups of water
- 2 ripe peaches, peeled, pitted, and diced
- 1 tsp ground cinnamon
- 2 tbsp honey (optional)

- 1/4 cup of chopped almonds (optional)
- Fresh mint leaves for garnish (optional)

Instructions

1. To get rid of any bitterness, give the quinoa a good rinse in cold water.
2. The washed quinoa and water should be put in a medium pot. Over medium-high heat, bring to a boil.
3. When the quinoa starts to boil, lower the heat to low, cover the pan, and simmer for 15 to 20 minutes, or until the quinoa is cooked and the water has been absorbed. Utilize a fork to fluff the quinoa.
4. Mix the chopped peaches and ground cinnamon in a separate little bowl.
5. After the quinoa has finished cooking, turn off the heat. Toss the quinoa with the cinnamon-spiced peaches in a gentle circular motion.
6. If preferred, add honey to the quinoa and peaches and mix thoroughly.
7. To add texture and crunch, sprinkle chopped almonds over the top.
8. If desired, add some fresh mint leaves as a garnish.
9. Enjoy the warm quinoa with peaches and cinnamon!

Nutritional Information (approximate values per serving)

Calories: 300 Fat: 5g Carbohydrates: 55g Protein: 8g Fiber: 7g

Multigrain Pancakes with Strawberry Sauce

Preparation Time: 10 minutes

Cooking Time: 15 minutes

Total Time: 25 minutes

Ingredients

- 1 cup of multigrain flour (can substitute with whole wheat flour)
- 1/2 cup of all-purpose flour
- 2 tbsp sugar
- 2 tsp baking powder
- 1/2 tsp baking soda
- 1/4 tsp salt
- 1 cup of buttermilk (can substitute with regular milk)
- 1/2 cup of Greek yogurt
- 2 large eggs
- 2 tbsp melted butter or oil
- 1 tsp vanilla extract

Strawberry Sauce

- 2 cups of fresh strawberries
- 2 tbsp sugar
- 1 tbsp lemon juice
- Optional toppings: sliced strawberries, powdered sugar, whipped cream

Instructions

1. Mix the multigrain flour, all-purpose flour, sugar, baking soda, salt, and baking powder in a large mixing basin.
2. Buttermilk, Greek yogurt, eggs, melted butter or oil, and vanilla extract should all be mixed in a separate basin.
3. After adding the liquid components, mix the dry ingredients only until they are barely blended. Avoid mixing a few lumps, OK.
4. Over medium heat, preheat a nonstick skillet or griddle.
5. For every pancake, ladle 1/4 cup of batter into the griddle. Cook until surface bubbles appear, turn, and cook for an additional 1 -2 minutes or until golden brown. Continue by using the remaining batter.
6. Make the strawberry sauce while the pancakes are cooking. Strawberries, sugar, and lemon juice should all be mixed together in a small pot. About 5-7 minutes will pass as the strawberries soften and release their juices while cooking over medium heat with occasional stirring. Take it off the fire and let it a minute to cool.
7. The strawberry mixture should be smooth after being pureed in a blender or immersion blender. To get rid of any seeds, you can pass the sauce through a fine-mesh sieve.
8. The strawberry sauce should be drizzled over the multigrain pancakes before serving. Add more strawberry slices, whipped cream, or powdered sugar as desired.
9. Enjoy your wonderful strawberry sauce-topped multigrain pancakes!

Nutritional Information (approximate values per serving, without optional toppings)

Calories: 300 Fat: 8g Carbohydrates: 49g Protein: 10g Fiber: 5g

Bowl of Guacamole and Mango with Black Beans

Ingredients

- 2 ripe avocados
- 1 ripe mango, peeled and diced
- 1 cup of cooked black beans
- 1/4 cup of diced red onion
- 1 jalapeño pepper, seeded and finely diced (optional)
- Juice of 1 lime
- 2 tbsp chopped fresh cilantro
- Salt and pepper as needed
- Tortilla chips or fresh veggies for serving

Instructions

1. Take the pits from the avocados by cutting them in half, then scoop the meat into a dish.
2. With a fork, mash the avocados until they are the desired consistency (chunky or smooth).
3. To the bowl, add the diced mango, cooked black beans, red onion, optional jalapeno pepper, lime juice, and chopped cilantro.
4. Mix everything together by gently folding it all together.
5. As needed, add salt and pepper to the food. Lime juice or cilantro can be adjusted as needed.
6. Serve the black beans, guacamole, and mango with Mexican chips or raw vegetables for dipping.

Nutritional Information (approximate values per serving)

Calories: 280 Fat: 15g Carbohydrates: 32g Protein: 9g Fiber: 12g

Chocolate Banana Oats

Cooking time: 10 minutes

Preparation time: 5 minutes

Ingredients

- 1 cup of rolled oats
- 2 cups of water
- 1 ripe banana, mashed
- 2 tbsp cocoa powder
- 1 tbsp honey or maple syrup (optional for sweetness)
- 1/4 tsp vanilla extract
- Pinch of salt
- Optional toppings: sliced banana, chopped nuts, chocolate chips

Instructions

1. Bring the water to a boil in a saucepan over medium heat.
2. Turn the heat down to low and stir in the rolled oats. Cook the oats until they have absorbed the majority of the water and are creamy for about 5 minutes, stirring regularly.
3. To the saucepan, add the mashed banana, cocoa powder, honey or maple syrup, vanilla extract, and salt (if used). To thoroughly incorporate all the ingredients, stir well.
4. Oats should be cooked for a further 2-3 minutes, stirring once or twice, or until the mixture thickens and the flavors are thoroughly mixed.
5. Turn off the heat and remove the pot. At this point, you may change the sweetness if you'd like by including extra honey or maple syrup.
6. The bowls should include the chocolate banana oats for added

taste and texture, garnish with sliced banana, chopped almonds, and a few chocolate chips.

Nutrition information (per serving)

Calories: 280 Carbohydrates: 59g Protein: 7g Fat: 4g Fiber: 9g

Homemade Granola

Cooking time: 30 minutes

Preparation time: 10 minutes

Ingredients

- 3 cups of rolled oats
- 1 cup of mixed nuts chopped
- 1/2 cup of shredded coconut
- 1/4 cup of honey or maple syrup
- 2 tbsp coconut oil or vegetable oil
- 1 tsp vanilla extract
- 1/2 tsp cinnamon
- 1/4 tsp salt
- 1 cup of dried fruits (such as cranberries, raisins, apricots), chopped (optional)

Instructions

1. Set your oven's temperature to 325 °F (163 °C). Used parchment paper to line a baking sheet or gently oil it.
2. The rolled oats, mixed nuts, coconut shreds, cinnamon, and salt should all be mixed in a large mixing dish. To spread the ingredients equally, thoroughly stir them.
3. Warm the coconut oil, vanilla extract, and honey or maple syrup in a small saucepan over low heat. Stir continuously until the mixture is well-mixed and smooth.
4. Over the dry ingredients, pour the heated honey or maple syrup mixture. Make sure the dry ingredients are uniformly covered by combining everything with a spoon or spatula.
5. On the baking sheet that has been prepared, spread the granola mixture out evenly.
6. To achieve even baking, toss the granola after every 10 minutes in the preheated oven for around 20 to 25 minutes or until it turns golden brown. Watch it carefully since it may easily transition from golden to burned.
7. Take the baked granola from the oven and allow it to cool fully on the baking sheet. As it cools, it will continue to crisp up.
8. After the granola has cooled, you can add the dried fruits if you choose.
9. The homemade granola may be kept at room temperature for up to two weeks in an airtight container.

Nutrition information (per 1/4 cup of serving)

Calories: 180 Carbohydrates: 19g Protein: 4g Fat: 11g Fiber: 3g Sugar: 6g

Nutritious Bagels

Cooking time: 20 minutes

Preparation time: 1 hour 30 minutes

Ingredients

- 2 cups of whole wheat flour
- 1 cup of all-purpose flour
- 2 tsp active dry yeast
- 1 tsp salt
- 1 tbsp honey or maple syrup
- 1 cup of warm water
- Optional toppings: sesame seeds, poppy seeds, dried onion flakes, grated cheese

Instructions

1. Mix the whole wheat flour, all-purpose flour, yeast, and salt in a large mixing basin. To thoroughly incorporate the dry ingredients, stir.
2. Melt the honey or maple syrup in a separate basin of heated water. Don't let the water become too hot since that will destroy the yeast. Wait a few minutes for the yeast to become active and foamy.
3. The yeast mixture should be added to the dry ingredients. As soon as the dough begins to come together, stir with a spoon.
4. Transfer the dough to a surface that has been lightly dusted with flour, and knead it for 10 to 15 minutes or until it is smooth and elastic.
5. The dough should be rolled into a ball and put in an oiled basin. It needs to rise in a warm place, covered with a clean kitchen towel
6. , for about an hour, or until it has doubled in size.
7. Fire up the oven to 425 degrees Fahrenheit (220 degrees Celsius). Prepare a baking sheet with parchment paper.
8. Once the dough has risen, you may release the trapped air by punching it down. Cut the dough in half so you have 8 pieces.
9. Make a ball out of one part of the dough. To create a bagel shape, gently expand the hole created by your thumb poking through the middle. Repeat with the other dough halves.
10. On the preheated baking sheet, put the formed bagels. Allow them to rest for 15 to 20 minutes.
11. Bring a large saucepan of water to a rolling boil. When the water is boiling, gently add a few bagels at a time and let them cook for 1-2 minutes on every side.
12. The boiled bagels should be taken out of the water using a slotted spoon and put back on the baking sheet. If desired, top the bagels with your preferred toppings.
13. The bagels should bake for 15 to 18 minutes in a preheated oven or until golden brown.
14. The bagels should be taken out of the oven after baking and let to cool on a wire rack.
15. Enjoy your wholesome handmade bagels with your preferred toppings or spreads!

Nutrition information (per bagel)

Calories: 220 Carbohydrates: 46g Protein: 8g Fat: 1g Fiber: 6g Sugar: 2g

Breakfast Oatmeal

Cooking time: 5 minutes

Preparation time: 5 minutes

Ingredients

- 1 cup of rolled oats
- 2 cups of water or milk (dairy or plant-based)
- Pinch of salt
- 1 tbsp honey or maple syrup (optional for sweetness)
- 1/2 tsp vanilla extract
- Optional toppings: sliced fruits, nuts, seeds, nut butter, cinnamon, etc.

Instructions

1. Bring the milk or water to a boil in a saucepan over medium heat.
2. Add the rolled oats and a dash of salt after stirring. Once the oats have absorbed the majority of the liquid and reached the required consistency, turn the heat down to low and simmer the mixture for about 5 minutes, stirring regularly. Cook the porridge for a few extra minutes if you want your breakfast thicker.
3. Turn off the heat and remove the pot. You may flavor it with vanilla essence and add honey or maple syrup for sweetness if you want. To blend, thoroughly stir.
4. Place the oatmeal in dishes for serving.
5. Add your preferred toppings, such as cinnamon, sliced fruits (such as bananas or berries), almonds, seeds, or nut butter.
6. Serve the oatmeal warm, and enjoy!

Nutrition information (per serving)

Calories: 150 Carbohydrates: 27g Protein: 5g Fat: 3g Fiber: 4g Sugar: 6g

Banana Oatmeal Cup

Cooking time: 20 minutes

Preparation time: 10 minutes

Ingredients

- 2 cups of rolled oats
- 2 ripe bananas, mashed
- 1/4 cup of honey or maple syrup
- 1/4 cup of milk (dairy or plant-based)
- 1 tsp vanilla extract
- 1/2 tsp cinnamon
- Pinch of salt
- Optional add-ins: chopped nuts, dried fruits, chocolate chips, etc.

Instructions

1. Turn on the oven to 350 °F. Using paper liners, grease or line a muffin pan.
2. The rolled oats, mashed bananas, honey or maple syrup, milk, vanilla extract, cinnamon, and salt should all be mixed in a big bowl. Make careful to completely incorporate all the components by mixing well.
3. Add any other ingredients, such as chopped nuts, dried fruit, or chocolate chips, if preferred. To uniformly distribute them throughout the mixture, stir.
4. Fill every cup in the muffin tray that has been prepared about 3/4 full with the oatmeal mixture.
5. The oatmeal cups should be baked in the preheated oven for about 20

minutes or until they are set and have a light golden brown top.

6. The oatmeal cups should cool for a few minutes after the muffin pan has been taken out of the oven. After that, gently take them out of the tin and place them on a wire rack to finish cooling.

7. The oatmeal cups can be served once they have cooled. They may be kept in the fridge for up to a week in an airtight container. They may be consumed cold or quickly heated in the microwave.

Nutrition information (per serving, makes 12 cups of)

Calories: 120 Carbohydrates: 24g Protein: 3g Fat: 2g Fiber: 3g Sugar: 10g

Peanut Butter Oats

Cooking time: 5 minutes

Preparation time: 5 minutes

Ingredients

- 1 cup of rolled oats
- 2 cups of water or milk (dairy or plant-based)
- Pinch of salt
- 2 tbsp peanut butter
- 1 tbsp honey or maple syrup (optional for sweetness)
- Optional toppings: sliced banana, chopped nuts, chocolate chips, a drizzle of honey

Instructions

1. Bring the milk or water to a boil in a saucepan over medium heat.

2. Add the rolled oats and a dash of salt after stirring. Once the oats have absorbed the majority of the liquid and reached the required consistency, turn the heat down to low and simmer the mixture for about 5 minutes, stirring regularly. Cook the porridge for a few extra minutes if you want your breakfast thicker.

3. Turn off the heat and remove the pot. Honey or maple syrup (if using) and peanut butter should be thoroughly mixed.

4. Place the peanut butter oats in dishes for dishing.

5. Add your preferred garnishes, such as sliced bananas, chopped nuts, chocolate chips, or a honey drizzle.

6. Enjoy the warm peanut butter oats by serving them!

Nutrition information (per serving)

Calories: 350 Carbohydrates: 43g Protein: 11gFat: 16g Fiber: 5g Sugar: 9g

Breakfast Pizza

Cooking time: 20 minutes

Preparation time: 15 minutes

Ingredients

- 1 pre-made pizza crust (or homemade dough)
- 1 cup of shredded mozzarella cheese
- 4 large eggs
- 4 slices bacon, cooked and crumbled
- 1/2 cup of diced bell peppers
- 1/4 cup of diced red onions
- 1/4 cup of chopped fresh spinach

- Salt and pepper as needed
- Optional toppings: sliced tomatoes, avocado, mushrooms, sausage, etc.

Instructions

1. Preheat your oven to 425°F, if using handmade dough or according to the directions on the pre-made pizza crust packaging.
2. On a floured surface, roll out the pizza dough to the appropriate thickness. Take the crust on a baking sheet or pizza stone.
3. Leave a thin border around the borders and cover the entire pizza dough with the shredded mozzarella cheese.
4. The eggs should be thoroughly mixed in a small basin. As needed, add salt and pepper to the food.
5. Spread the beaten eggs equally over the cheese over the pizza dough.
6. Over the eggs, distribute the crumbled bacon, diced bell pepper, diced red onion, and chopped spinach.
7. Add any other toppings, such as sliced tomatoes, avocado, mushrooms, or sausage, as preferred.
8. The morning pizza should be baked for 12-15 minutes, or until the dough is golden brown and the eggs are set, in a preheated oven.
9. Before slicing, take the pizza out of the oven and let it cool for a while.
10. Enjoy breakfast pizza while it's still warm!

Nutrition information (per serving, makes 4 servings

Calories: 350 Carbohydrates: 25g Protein: 19g Fat: 19g

Breakfast Wraps

Cooking time: 15 minutes

Preparation time: 10 minutes

Ingredients

- 4 large flour tortillas (8-10 inches in diameter)
- 4 large eggs
- 1/4 cup of milk (dairy or plant-based)
- 1/2 cup of shredded cheddar cheese
- 4 slices cooked bacon, crumbled
- 1/2 cup of diced bell peppers
- 1/4 cup of diced red onions
- Salt and pepper as needed
- Optional toppings: avocado slices, salsa, hot sauce, sour cream

Instructions

1. Whisk the eggs and milk together in a medium bowl. As needed, add salt and pepper to the food.
2. A little butter or oil should be heated in a non-stick pan over medium heat. Pour the beaten eggs into the skillet and scramble them until they are fully cooked, stirring periodically. Get rid of the heat.
3. To make the flour tortillas more malleable, reheat them in the microwave or on a griddle.
4. The scrambled eggs should be evenly distributed among the tortillas, sitting in the middle of everyone.
5. Every tortilla's scrambled eggs should be covered with shredded cheddar cheese, crumbled bacon, chopped bell peppers, and diced red onions.

6. Add any additional toppings, such as avocado slices, salsa, spicy sauce, or sour cream, as preferred.
7. Every tortilla is made into a wrap by folding the edges inside and rolling it up firmly from the bottom.
8. An optional step is to preheat a pan or griddle. Grease the surface just a little bit with oil or butter. Seam side down, place the wraps in the skillet and cook for 2-3 minutes on every side or until the cheese has melted and the tortillas are gently toasted. Although it is optional, this step may give the wraps a lovely crispness.
9. Before serving, take the wraps out of the skillet and let them cool for a while.
10. Enjoy the breakfast wraps while they're still warm!

Nutrition information (per serving, makes 4 servings)

Calories: 340 Carbohydrates: 26g Protein: 17g Fat: 19g Fiber: 2g Sugar: 2g

Portobello Mushrooms Florentine

Cooking time: 20 minutes

Preparation time: 15 minutes

Ingredients

- 4 large Portobello mushrooms
- 2 cups of fresh spinach leaves
- 1/2 cup of shredded mozzarella cheese
- 1/4 cup of grated Parmesan cheese
- 2 tbsp olive oil
- 2 cloves garlic, minced

- 1/4 tsp red pepper flakes (optional)
- Salt and pepper as needed

Instructions

1. Set your oven's temperature to 375°F (190°C). A baking sheet should be lightly greased or lined with parchment paper.
2. Use a paper towel or moist cloth to wipe the Portobello mushrooms clean. After removing the stems, carefully scrape out the mushroom's gills with a spoon.
3. Olive oil should be heated in a pan over medium heat. Red pepper flakes (if used) and chopped garlic are added, and they are cooked for approximately a minute until aromatic.
4. Cook fresh spinach leaves in the pan for two to three minutes until they wilt. As needed, add salt and pepper to the food.
5. Place the Portobello mushrooms, gill side up, on the prepared baking sheet. Fill the spaces in every mushroom with an equal amount of sautéed spinach.
6. Over the spinach in every mushroom, smear some grated Parmesan and mozzarella cheese.
7. Bake until the cheese is melted and bubbling and the mushrooms have softened about 15 minutes.
8. Before serving, take the mushrooms out of the oven and let them cool for a while.
9. The Portobello Mushrooms Florentine is a tasty and wholesome main dish or appetizer.

Nutrition information (per serving, makes 4 servings)

Calories: 150 Carbohydrates: 7g Protein: 9g
Fat: 11g Fiber: 2g Sugar: 2g

Peanut Butter Oatmeal

Cooking time: 5 minutes

Preparation time: 5 minutes

Ingredients

- 1 cup of rolled oats
- 2 cups of water or milk (dairy or plant-based)
- Pinch of salt
- 2 tbsp peanut butter
- 1 tbsp honey or maple syrup (optional for sweetness)
- Optional toppings: sliced banana, chopped nuts, chocolate chips, a drizzle of honey

Instructions

1. Bring the milk or water to a boil in a saucepan over medium heat.
2. Add the rolled oats and a dash of salt after stirring. Once the oats have absorbed the majority of the liquid and reached the required consistency, turn the heat down to low and simmer the mixture for about 5 minutes, stirring regularly. Cook the porridge for a few extra minutes if you want your breakfast thicker.
3. Turn off the heat and remove the pot. Honey or maple syrup (if using) and peanut butter should be thoroughly mixed.
4. Place the oats with peanut butter in the dishes for dishing.

5. Add your preferred garnishes, such as sliced bananas, chopped nuts, chocolate chips, or a honey drizzle.
6. Enjoy the warm peanut butter oatmeal by serving it!

Nutrition information (per serving)

Calories: 350 Carbohydrates: 45g Protein: 13g Fat: 14g Fiber: 7g Sugar: 10g

Chia Seed Parfaits

Preparation time: 10 minutes

Chilling time: 2-3 hours or overnight

Ingredients

- 1/4 cup of chia seeds
- 1 cup of milk (dairy or plant-based)
- 1 tbsp honey or maple syrup
- 1/2 tsp vanilla extract
- 1 cup of Greek yogurt
- 1 cup of mixed berries
- Optional toppings: granola, shredded coconut, chopped nuts, additional berries

Instructions

1. Chia seeds, milk, honey or maple syrup, and vanilla extract should all be mixed in a mixing dish. Stir the mixture thoroughly to make sure the chia seeds are dispersed equally throughout.
2. To avoid clumping, give the mixture another stir after letting it settle for a few minutes. To make sure the chia seeds are thoroughly mixed in and don't clump together, repeat this procedure a few times over the course of 15 minutes.

3. Chia seed mixture should be chilled for at least two to three hours or, better yet, overnight. Cover the bowl. This will make it possible for the chia seeds to absorb the liquid and take on the consistency of pudding.
4. It's time to put the parfaits together when the chia seed mixture has thickened and set.
5. Layer the chia seed pudding and Greek yogurt alternately in serving jars or glasses. Greek yogurt is placed on top of the first layer of chia seed pudding, and so on, until all of the glasses or jars are full.
6. Add plenty of mixed berries and any additional preferred toppings, such as granola, coconut flakes, or chopped almonds, to every parfait.
7. For a further 30 minutes of chilling and flavor melding, place the parfaits in the refrigerator.
8. Enjoy the cooled chia seed parfaits after serving!

Nutrition information (per serving)

Calories: 280 Carbohydrates: 34g Protein: 16g Fat: 10g Fiber: 12g Sugar: 17g

Breakfast Tacos

Cooking time: 15 minutes

Preparation time: 10 minutes

Ingredients

- 4 small flour tortillas (6-8 inches in diameter)
- 4 large eggs
- 1 tbsp olive oil
- 1/2 cup of diced bell peppers
- 1/4 cup of diced red onions
- 1/2 cup of cooked black beans
- 1/2 cup of shredded cheddar cheese
- Salt and pepper as needed
- Optional toppings: salsa, avocado slices, sour cream, chopped cilantro

Instructions

1. Over medium heat, warm the olive oil in a skillet.
2. Diced red onions and bell peppers should be added to the skillet. 3 to 4 minutes of sautéing is sufficient to soften them mildly.
3. The eggs should be thoroughly mixed in a basin. As needed, add salt and pepper to the food.
4. Move the onions and bell peppers that have been sautéed to one side of the pan. The opposite side of the skillet should now contain the beaten eggs, which you should scramble until fully done.
5. When the eggs are done, add them to the skillet along with the onions and bell peppers that have been sautéed. Mix in the cooked black beans after adding everything else.
6. To make the flour tortillas more malleable, reheat them in the microwave or grill.
7. Place an equal amount of the egg and veggie mixture in the center of every tortilla.
8. Over every tortilla's contents, scatter some shredded cheddar cheese.
9. Add toppings, such as salsa, avocado slices, sour cream, or chopped cilantro.
10. Every tortilla is folded in half lengthwise and then firmly rolled up from the bottom to create a taco.
11. Enjoy breakfast tacos while they're still warm!

Nutrition information (per serving, makes 4 servings)

Calories: 300 Carbohydrates: 25g Protein: 15g Fat: 16g Fiber: 5g Sugar: 2g

Spring Vegetable Frittata

Cooking time: 25 minutes

Preparation time: 15 minutes

Ingredients

- 8 large eggs
- 1/4 cup of milk (dairy or plant-based)
- 1 tbsp olive oil
- 1 small onion, diced
- 2 cloves garlic, minced
- 1 cup of sliced asparagus
- 1 cup of sliced zucchini
- 1 cup of halved cherry tomatoes
- 1/2 cup of fresh spinach leaves
- 1/2 cup of crumbled feta cheese
- Salt and pepper as needed
- Fresh herbs for garnish (such as parsley or chives)

Instructions

1. Preheat your oven to 375°F.
2. Mix the milk and eggs in a bowl until fully mixed. As needed, add salt and pepper to the food. Place aside.
3. In an oven-safe skillet set over medium heat, warm the olive oil. Sauté the minced garlic and chopped onion for 2 to 3 minutes or until aromatic and softening.
4. Sliced zucchini and asparagus should be added to the skillet. After another 4-5 minutes of sautéing, the veggies should be crisp-tender.
5. Cherry tomatoes, cut in half, and new spinach leaves should be added to the skillet. Cook the spinach for 1-2 minutes or until it begins to wilt.
6. Over the skillet's sautéed veggies, pour the egg mixture. To spread the veggies evenly, gently stir.
7. On top of the frittata, scatter the feta cheese crumbles.
8. When the frittata is set and the top is faintly brown, place the pan in the oven and bake for 15-18 minutes.
9. After removing the pan from the oven, give the frittata some time to cool.
10. Before slicing and serving, garnish with fresh herbs, such as parsley or chives.
11. The Spring Vegetable Frittata can be served hot or cold. It is suitable for every meal, including brunch and breakfast.

Nutrition information (per serving, makes 6 servings)

Calories: 180 Carbohydrates: 6g Protein: 12g Fat: 13g Fiber: 1g Sugar: 3g

Asparagus, Salmon, and Tomato Quiche

Preparation time: 20 minutes

Cooking time: 35-40 minutes

Ingredients

- 1 pre-made pie crust (9-inch)
- 1 cup of asparagus spears, trimmed and cut into 1-inch pieces
- 4 oz. cooked salmon, flaked
- 1/2 cup of cherry tomatoes, halved
- 1 cup of shredded Swiss cheese
- 4 large eggs
- 1 cup of milk (dairy or plant-based)
- 1/4 tsp salt
- 1/4 tsp black pepper
- 1/4 tsp dried dill (optional)
- Fresh dill sprigs for garnish (optional)

Instructions

1. Preheat your oven to 375°F.
2. Press the pre-made pie crust firmly into the bottom and up the sides of a 9-inch pie plate. If needed, remove any extra crust.
3. Water should be brought to a boil in a medium-sized saucepan. Asparagus spears are added, and they are blanched for 2 minutes. To halt the cooking process, drain and rinse them with cold water.
4. Sprinkle the blanched asparagus, cherry tomato halves, and flakes salmon over the pie shell in a uniform layer.
5. In a mixing dish, thoroughly mix the eggs, milk, salt, pepper, and dried dill (if using).
6. The egg mixture will cover the salmon and veggies in the pie shell.
7. Swiss cheese that has been shredded is added on top.
8. When the top is golden brown and the middle has set, place the quiche in the oven and bake for 36-40 minutes.
9. The quiche should be removed from the oven and allowed to cool before cutting.
10. Before serving, if preferred, garnish with fresh dill sprigs.
11. Warm or room-temperature servings of the asparagus, salmon, and tomato quiche are OK. It's a fantastic alternative for brunch, supper, or a light meal.

Nutrition information (per serving, makes 6 servings)

Calories: 340 Carbohydrates: 17g Protein: 19gFat: 21g Fiber: 1g Sugar: 3g

Sausage and Egg Sandwich

Preparation time: 5 minutes

Cooking time: 15 minutes

Ingredients

- 4 breakfast sausage patties
- 4 large eggs
- 4 slices of cheese (cheddar, Swiss, or your preferred type)
- 4 English muffins or burger buns
- 1 tbsp butter or oil
- Salt and pepper as needed
- Optional toppings: sliced tomatoes, avocado, lettuce, ketchup, mayonnaise

Instructions

1. Set your oven's temperature to 400°F (200°C). The sausage patties should be baked for 10-12 minutes or until thoroughly cooked, as directed on the packaging, before being placed on a baking sheet.
2. Butter or oil should be heated to a medium-high temperature in a pan.
3. One at a time, crack every egg into the skillet. Add pepper and salt as needed when seasoning. Scramble, over-easy, or cook the eggs to your preferred level of doneness.
4. Cut the English muffins or hamburger buns in half while the eggs cook. Your choice for toasting them.
5. When the sausage patties are done cooking, take them out of the oven and press any extra oil dry with a paper towel.
6. Place a piece on top of every sausage patty to gently melt the cheese.
7. Place one cooked sausage patty with cheese on the bottom half of every English muffin or bun to assemble the sandwiches.
8. On top of the sausage patty, place a cooked egg.
9. Any preferred toppings, such as lettuce, sliced tomatoes, avocados, ketchup, or mayonnaise, may be added.
10. The sandwich is finished by adding the top half of the English muffin or bun.
11. The sausage and egg sandwiches are best served warm, so do so immediately.

Nutrition information (per sandwich)

Calories: 450 Carbohydrates: 26g Protein: 25g Fat: 28g Fiber: 2g Sugar: 3g

Tomato Egg Tart

Preparation time: 15 minutes

Cooking time: 25-30 minutes

Ingredients

- 1 pre-made pie crust (9-inch)
- 4 large eggs
- 1/2 cup of milk
- 1 cup of cherry tomatoes, halved
- 1/2 cup of shredded mozzarella cheese
- 1/4 cup of grated Parmesan cheese
- 2 tbsp chopped fresh basil
- Salt and pepper as needed

Instructions

1. Preheat your oven to 375°F.
2. Press pre-made pie crust into a 9-inch tart pan. If needed, remove any extra crust.
3. Eggs, milk, salt, and pepper should all be thoroughly incorporated into a mixing dish.
4. Distribute the cherry tomato halves evenly on the tart crust's bottom.
5. The tomatoes in the tart crust will be covered with the egg mixture.
6. Over the egg mixture, smear the grated Parmesan and mozzarella cheese.
7. On top of the cheese, sprinkle the fresh basil, chopped.
8. When the center is set, and the top is golden, place the tomato egg tart in the oven and bake for 25-30 minutes.

9. The tart should be removed from the oven and allowed to cool before cutting.
10. The Tomato Egg Tart can be served warm or at room temperature. It tastes well as a breakfast, brunch, or light lunch.

Nutrition information (per serving, makes 6 servings)

Calories: 260 Carbohydrates: 16g Protein: 11g Fat: 17g Fiber: 1g Sugar: 2g

Spinach Wraps

Preparation time: 10 minutes

Cooking time: 0 minutes

Ingredients

- 4 large spinach tortillas (8-10 inches in diameter)
- 1 cup of cooked quinoa
- 1 cup of fresh spinach leaves
- 1/2 cup of diced bell peppers
- 1/4 cup of diced red onions
- 1/4 cup of crumbled feta cheese
- 2 tbsp hummus or your preferred spread
- Salt and pepper as needed

Instructions

1. On a spotless board, spread out the tortillas with spinach.
2. Every tortilla should have a small coating of hummus or any chosen spread applied to it, leaving a border all the way around.
3. The cooked quinoa, fresh spinach leaves, chopped bell peppers, diced red onions, and feta cheese are all mixed in a dish. As needed, add salt

and pepper to the food. Mix thoroughly.
4. After evenly dividing it, place a small amount of the quinoa mixture in the middle of every tortilla.
5. Every tortilla is made into a wrap by folding the edges inside and rolling it up firmly from the bottom.
6. If preferred, cut the wraps in half before serving.
7. Enjoy your wholesome and tasty spinach wraps!

Nutrition information (per wrap)

Calories: 260 Carbohydrates: 35g Protein: 9g Fat: 9g Fiber: 6g Sugar: 3g

Vegetable Shake

Preparation time: 5 minutes

Cooking time: 0 minutes

Ingredients

- 1 cup of spinach leaves
- 1 small cucumber, peeled and chopped
- 1 medium carrot, peeled and chopped
- 1 celery stalk, chopped
- 1/2 green apple, cored and chopped
- 1/2 lemon, juiced
- 1 cup of unsweetened almond milk
- Optional: 1 tbsp chia seeds or flaxseeds

Instructions

1. Put all the ingredients in a food processor or blender.
2. Blend at a high speed until the mixture is fully blended and smooth.

3. If preferred, Chia seeds or flaxseeds can be added to the blender; mix for 10 to 15 seconds.
4. The veggie shake should be poured into a glass and served right away.
5. Enjoy your refreshing and nutritious Vegetable Shake!

Nutrition information (per serving)

Calories: 100 Carbohydrates: 18g Protein: 4g Fat: 2g Fiber: 5g Sugar: 9g

Cashew Nut Shake

Preparation time: 5 minutes

Cooking time: 0 minutes

Ingredients

- 1/2 cup of raw cashews
- 2 cups of water
- 2 tbsp honey or maple syrup
- 1/2 tsp vanilla extract
- Pinch of salt
- Ice cubes (optional for a chilled shake)

Instructions

1. Put the raw cashews in a dish and add water to cover them. Give them at least 4 hours or maybe the entire night to soak. The cashews will get softer, making them simpler to mix.
2. Drain and rinse the cashews after soaking.
3. The soaked cashews, water, honey or maple syrup (if used), vanilla extract, and a dash of salt should all be mixed in a blender.
4. Blend the ingredients at a high speed until it becomes creamy and smooth.

5. If desired, add a few ice cubes to the blender and blitz one more until everything is well mixed. The shake will have a cold and revitalizing consistency as a result.
6. The cashew nut shake should be poured into a glass and served immediately.
7. Take pleasure in your luscious Cashew Nut Shake.

Nutrition information (per serving)

Calories: 250 Carbohydrates: 18g Protein: 6g Fat: 18g Fiber: 2g Sugar: 6g

Hummus and Date Bagels

Preparation time: 5 minutes

Cooking time: 0 minutes

Ingredients

- 2 bagels (your choice of flavor)
- 1/2 cup of hummus (store-bought or homemade)
- 4 Medjool dates, pitted and sliced
- Optional toppings: arugula, micro greens, sliced cucumbers

Instructions

1. The bagels should be cut in half horizontally.
2. Every bagel's bottom half should have a thick layer of hummus on it.
3. Spread out the cut dates equally over the top of the hummus.
4. Add toppings like arugula, micro greens, or thinly sliced cucumbers if preferred.
5. To finish the sandwich, place the top half of the bagel on the filling.

6. Serve the date bagels and hummus right away.
7. Enjoy your tasty, healthy bagel sandwich!

Nutrition information (per serving)

Calories: 350 Carbohydrates: 68g Protein: 11g Fat: 6g Fiber: 7g Sugar: 31g

Curry Tofu Scramble

Preparation time: 10 minutes

Cooking time: 15 minutes

Ingredients

- 1 tbsp oil (such as olive oil or coconut oil)
- 1 small onion, diced
- 2 cloves garlic, minced
- 1 red bell pepper, diced
- 1 tbsp curry powder
- 1/2 tsp ground cumin
- 1/2 tsp ground turmeric
- 1/4 tsp paprika
- 1/4 tsp salt
- 1/4 tsp black pepper
- 1 block (14 oz) firm tofu, drained and crumbled
- 1 cup of fresh spinach leaves
- 2 green onions, sliced
- Optional toppings: chopped cilantro, sliced tomatoes, hot sauce

Instructions

1. In a big skillet over medium heat, warm the oil.
2. Add the diced red bell pepper, minced garlic, and chopped onion to the pan. To soften the veggies, sauté for around 5 minutes.
3. Mix the curry powder, cumin, turmeric, paprika, salt, and black pepper in a small bowl.
4. Add the spice mixture and the crushed tofu to the skillet. Stir thoroughly to coat the tofu and distribute the seasonings equally.
5. The tofu mixture should be cooked through and start to brown after approximately 7-8 minutes of cooking while stirring occasionally.
6. When the spinach wilts, add the fresh leaves to the pan and simmer for 2 minutes.
7. Sliced green onions should be added to the tofu scramble after the pan has removed the heat.
8. With optional toppings like chopped cilantro, sliced tomatoes, or spicy sauce, serve the curry tofu scramble hot.
9. Take pleasure in your tasty and nutrient-dense Curry Tofu Scramble.

Nutrition information (per serving)

Calories: 220 Carbohydrates: 12g Protein: 17g Fat: 12g Fiber: 5g Sugar: 4g

Egg Foo Young

Preparation time: 15 minutes

Cooking time: 15 minutes

Ingredients

For the omelets

- 4 large eggs
- 1/4 cup of diced onion
- 1/4 cup of diced bell peppers
- 1/4 cup of diced mushrooms
- 1/4 cup of bean sprouts
- 2 tbsp chopped green onions

- 1 tbsp soy sauce
- 1/2 tsp sesame oil
- Salt and pepper as needed
- Cooking oil for frying

For the gravy:

- 1 cup of chicken or vegetable broth
- 1 tbsp soy sauce
- 1 tbsp oyster sauce
- 1 tbsp cornstarch
- 1/4 cup of water

Instructions

1. Eggs, chopped onion, bell pepper, mushroom, bean sprouts, green onions, soy sauce, sesame oil, salt, and pepper should all be well blended in a dish before adding other ingredients.
2. A nonstick frying pan or skillet is heated over medium heat with a minimal quantity of cooking oil.
3. Form a circle omelet in the skillet by pouring half of the egg mixture. Cook for 2 to 3 minutes or until the bottom is firm and browned.
4. Use a spatula to flip the omelet gently, then cook the opposite side for two to three minutes. Take out of the skillet and place aside. Make a second omelet with the remaining egg mixture by repeating the procedure.
5. Mix the chicken or vegetable broth, soy sauce, and oyster sauce in a small pot. Over medium heat, bring to a simmer.
6. Cornstarch and water should be mixed to make a slurry in a different bowl. Stirring continuously, gradually incorporate the slurry into the boiling sauce as it thickens. Eliminate heat.

7. Fold one omelet in half and set it on a dish to serve. Over the omelet, spoon some of the gravy.
8. Make a second omelet as before. Add more green onions as a garnish, if desired.
9. Serve hot Egg Foo Young for a tasty and filling dinner.

Nutrition information (per serving, makes 2 servings)

Calories: 280 Carbohydrates: 13g Protein: 18g Fat: 17g Fiber: 2g Sugar: 4g

Cranberry Hotcakes

Preparation time: 10 minutes

Cooking time: 10 minutes

Ingredients

- 1 cup of all-purpose flour
- 2 tbsp sugar
- 1 tsp baking powder
- 1/2 tsp baking soda
- 1/4 tsp salt
- 1/2 cup of dried cranberries
- 1 cup of buttermilk
- 1 large egg
- 2 tbsp unsalted butter, melted
- 1/2 tsp vanilla extract
- Cooking oil or butter for greasing the pan

Instructions

1. Mix the flour, baking soda, salt, baking powder, sugar in a large dish.
2. The dried cranberries should be thoroughly mixed in.

3. Mix the buttermilk, egg, melted butter, and vanilla extract in a separate basin.
4. After adding the liquid components, mix the dry ingredients by gently combining them. Avoid over-mixing; a few lumps are OK.
5. A nonstick griddle or skillet should be heated to medium. Grease the surface just a little bit with butter or cooking oil.
6. For every hotcake, pour roughly 1/4 cup of the batter into the hot skillet. To create a spherical shape, gently spread the batter using the back of a spoon.
7. The hotcakes should be cooked on the first side for two to three minutes or until bubbles appear on the top.
8. Hotcakes should be turned over and fried for two to three minutes on the other side or until golden brown and thoroughly done.
9. Hotcakes should be taken out of the skillet and kept warm. With the remaining batter, repeat the procedure.
10. Warm Cranberry Hotcakes can be served with whipped cream, maple syrup, or more dried cranberries.
11. Enjoy your tasty and fluffy cranberry pancakes!

Nutrition information (per serving, makes about 8 hotcakes)

Calories: 160 Carbohydrates: 26g Protein: 4g Fat: 5g Fiber: 1g Sugar: 10g

CHAPTER 2: LUNCH RECIPES

Turkey Keema Curry

Preparation time: 10 minutes

Cooking time: 25 minutes

Ingredients

- 1 tbsp vegetable oil
- 1 onion, finely chopped
- 2 cloves garlic, minced
- 1 tbsp ginger, grated
- 1 green chilli, finely chopped (optional; adjust to your spice preference)
- 1 lb. ground turkey
- 1 tsp ground cumin
- 1 tsp ground coriander
- 1/2 tsp turmeric powder
- 1/2 tsp red chilli powder
- 1/2 tsp garam masala
- 1 cup of diced tomatoes (canned or fresh)
- 1/2 cup of frozen peas
- Salt as need
- Fresh cilantro for garnish

Instructions

1. Warm the vegetable oil over medium heat in a large skillet or pan.
2. The chopped onion should be added and sautéed for about 5 minutes or until transparent.
3. Add the chopped green chile, grated ginger, and minced garlic if using. Cook until fragrant for a further 1-2 minutes.

4. With a spatula, crumble the ground turkey into the pan. Cook the turkey until it is well done and browned.
5. The skillet should now include red chilli powder, ground cumin, coriander, turmeric powder, and garam masala. The spices should be properly mixed to coat the turkey.
6. To the skillet, add the diced tomatoes and frozen peas. To blend, stir.
7. To let the flavors merge, boil the heat to low and simmer the mixture for 10 to 15 minutes. Sometimes stir.
8. As needed, add salt to the dish.
9. Add fresh cilantro as a garnish.
10. Warm rice or naan bread should be served with the turkey keema curry.
11. Take pleasure in your tasty and nutrient-dense Turkey Keema Curry.

Nutrition information (per serving, makes about 4 servings)

Calories: 250 Carbohydrates: 9g Protein: 25g Fat: 13g Fiber: 2g Sugar: 4g

Orzo, Bean, and Tuna Salad

Preparation time: 15 minutes

Cooking time: 10 minutes

Ingredients

- 8 oz. orzo pasta
- 1 can (15 oz.) cannellini beans, drained and rinsed
- 1 can (5 oz.) tuna, drained
- 1 cup of cherry tomatoes, halved
- 1/2 cup of diced cucumber
- 1/4 cup of chopped red onion
- 1/4 cup of chopped fresh parsley
- 2 tbsp extra-virgin olive oil
- 2 tbsp lemon juice
- 1 garlic clove, minced
- Salt and pepper as needed

Instructions

1. To prepare the orzo pasta, follow the directions on the package. Drain, then leave to cool.
2. The cooked orzo pasta, cannellini beans, tuna, cherry tomatoes, sliced cucumber, chopped red onion, and chopped parsley should all be mixed in a big bowl.
3. Mix the extra virgin olive oil, minced garlic, salt, lemon juice, and pepper in a separate small bowl to create the dressing.
4. As you pour the dressing over the orzo mixture, gently toss everything to distribute it evenly.
5. If necessary, add extra salt and pepper after tasting the food.
6. For the flavors to mix, let the salad cool in the refrigerator for at least 30 minutes.
7. We serve the cold orzo, bean, and tuna salad as a light and satiating lunch.
8. Enjoy your savory and filling salad!

Nutrition information (per serving, makes about 4 servings)

Calories: 400 Carbohydrates: 54g Protein: 21g Fat: 11g Fiber: 9g Sugar: 3g

Smoked Haddock and Spinach Rye Toasts

Preparation time: 10 minutes

Cooking time: 15 minutes

Ingredients

- 4 slices of rye bread
- 8 oz. smoked haddock fillets
- 2 cups of fresh spinach leaves
- 1 small onion, thinly sliced
- 1 garlic clove, minced
- 2 tbsp olive oil
- 2 tbsp lemon juice
- 1 tbsp chopped fresh dill (optional)
- Salt and pepper as needed

Instructions

1. Turn on the oven to 400 °F.
2. Haddock fillets that have been smoked should be put on a foil-lined baking pan. Add a squeeze of lemon juice, 1 tbsp of olive oil, and salt & pepper as needed.
3. Haddock fillets should be baked in the oven for 12 to 15 minutes or until well cooked and readily flaked with a fork.
4. The remaining 1 tbsp of olive oil should be warmed in a pan over medium heat while the haddock roasts. Add the minced garlic and thinly sliced onion, and cook for 3 to 4 minutes or until tender and transparent.
5. Fresh spinach leaves should be added to the pan and cooked for two to three minutes or until they wilt.
6. Slices of rye bread should be crisp and golden when toasted.

7. Take the cooked haddock out of the oven, then flake it into bite-sized pieces.
8. The sautéed spinach and onion combination should be placed on top of every piece of toasted rye bread. The flakes of smoked haddock should then be added.
9. Garnish with freshly chopped dill, if preferred.
10. Warm up the Smoked Haddock and Spinach Rye Toasts to serve as a tasty and wholesome starter or quick lunch.
11. Enjoy your tasty, high-protein toast!

Nutrition information (per serving, makes about 4 toasts)

Calories: 280 Carbohydrates: 21g Protein: 22g Fat: 11g Fiber: 3g Sugar: 2g

Chipotle Chicken Lunch Wraps

Preparation time: 10 minutes

Cooking time: 15 minutes

Ingredients

- 2 large flour tortillas (10-inch)
- 2 boneless, skinless chicken breasts
- 1 tbsp chipotle seasoning (or as needed)
- 1 tbsp olive oil
- 1/2 cup of diced tomatoes
- 1/4 cup of diced red onion
- 1/4 cup of diced bell peppers
- 1/4 cup of canned black beans, rinsed and drained
- 1/4 cup of shredded cheddar cheese

- 1/4 cup of sour cream or Greek yogurt
- Fresh cilantro leaves for garnish (optional)

Instructions

1. Heat your skillet or grill to medium-high.
2. Apply chipotle spice evenly on both sides of the chicken breasts.
3. On top of the seasoned chicken breasts, drizzle some olive oil.
4. The chicken should be cooked through after 6 to 8 minutes on every side of the grill or in a pan. Cooking time depends on chicken breast thickness. Make sure the inside is 165°F (74°C) or above.
5. After the chicken has finished cooking, please turn off the heat and give it time to rest. After that, cut it into tiny pieces.
6. On a spotless board, spread out the flour tortillas.
7. The chicken should be evenly divided and positioned in the middle of every tortilla.
8. Add chopped tomatoes, diced red onion, bell peppers, black beans, shredded cheddar cheese, sour cream, or Greek yogurt to the top of the chicken.
9. Garnish with fresh cilantro leaves, if preferred.
10. Every tortilla is made into a wrap by folding the edges inside and then securely rolling it up from the bottom.
11. If preferred, cut the wraps in half before serving.
12. Take pleasure in your savory and nutrient-dense Chipotle Chicken Lunch Wraps!

Nutrition information (per wrap)

Calories: 450 Carbohydrates: 33g Protein: 30g Fat: 20g Fiber: 5g Sugar: 3g

Salmon with Marinade

Preparation time: 10 minutes

Marinating time: 30 minutes

Cooking time: 12-15 minutes

Ingredients

- 2 salmon fillets (6 oz. every)
- 2 tbsp soy sauce
- 2 tbsp honey or maple syrup
- 2 tbsp olive oil
- 2 cloves garlic, minced
- 1 tbsp freshly squeezed lemon juice
- 1/2 tsp ground black pepper
- Optional garnish: chopped fresh parsley or dill

Instructions

1. Mix the soy sauce, honey or maple syrup, olive oil, garlic powder, lemon juice, and black pepper in a small bowl to make the marinade.
2. Put the salmon fillets in a sealable plastic bag or a shallow plate.
3. As you pour the marinade over the salmon, coat it completely. Seal the plastic bag if you're using it, then rub the salmon with the marinade.
4. Marinate the salmon in the fridge for at least 30 minutes to allow the flavors to permeate the fish.
5. Turn on the oven to 400 °F. Used foil or parchment paper to line a baking sheet.
6. Place the skin-side-down salmon fillets marinated on the prepared

baking sheet. Any leftover marinade should be applied to the fish.

7. Salmon should be baked for 12 to 15 minutes or until well cooked and flaked with a fork. Depending on fillet thickness, cooking durations may vary.
8. The salmon should be taken out of the oven and rested.
9. If desired, garnish with finely chopped fresh parsley or dill.
10. Serve the heated salmon with marinade as a tasty and wholesome supper.
11. Take pleasure in your tasty, high-protein salmon!

Nutrition information (per serving, based on 6-oz. salmon fillets)

Calories: 350 Carbohydrates: 14g Protein: 34g Fat: 19g Fiber: 0g Sugar: 12g

Balsamic Roast Chicken

Preparation time: 10 minutes

Marinating time: 30 minutes (optional)

Cooking time: 40-45 minutes

Ingredients

- 4 chicken drumsticks
- 4 chicken thighs
- 1/4 cup of balsamic vinegar
- 2 tbsp olive oil
- 2 tbsp honey
- 4 cloves garlic, minced
- 1 tsp dried rosemary
- 1 tsp dried thyme
- 1/2 tsp salt
- 1/4 tsp black pepper

- Optional garnish: Fresh parsley or thyme sprigs

Instructions

1. To make the marinade, mix the balsamic vinegar, olive oil, honey, minced garlic, dried thyme, dried rosemary, salt, and pepper in a bowl.
2. Place the chicken thighs and drumsticks in a shallow dish or a plastic bag that can be sealed.
3. To ensure the chicken is well covered, pour the marinade over it. Seal the plastic bag if you're using it, then massage the chicken with the marinade. Refrigerate the food in the marinade for at least 30 minutes or even overnight if you choose.
4. Turn on the oven to 425 °F. Used foil or parchment paper to line a baking sheet.
5. Place the skin-side-up, marinated chicken pieces on the prepared baking sheet. Any leftover marinade should be poured over the chicken.
6. For 40 to 45 minutes, or until the chicken is cooked and the skin is crispy and browned, roast the chicken in the oven. The chicken cooked to an internal temperature of 165°F (74°C).
7. After removing the chicken from the oven, give it some time to rest.
8. If preferred, garnish with fresh sprigs of thyme or parsley.
9. Balsamic Roast Chicken should be served hot for a tasty and filling supper.
10. Enjoy your juicy and delicious roast chicken!

Nutrition information

Calories: 380 Carbohydrates: 10g Protein: 25g Fat: 26g Fiber: 0g Sugar: 9g

Salad with Balsamic Vinaigrette

Preparation time: 10 minutes

Cooking time: 0 minutes

Ingredients

For the Salad

- 6 cups of mixed salad greens (such as romaine lettuce, spinach, or arugula)
- 1 cup of cherry tomatoes, halved
- 1/2 cup of sliced cucumbers
- 1/4 cup of thinly sliced red onions
- 1/4 cup of crumbled feta cheese
- 1/4 cup of chopped walnuts or almonds (optional)
- Optional additional toppings: sliced avocado, boiled eggs, grilled chicken breast

Ingredients for the Balsamic Vinaigrette

- 3 tbsp balsamic vinegar
- 2 tbsp extra-virgin olive oil
- 1 tsp Dijon mustard
- 1 tsp honey or maple syrup
- 1 clove garlic, minced
- Salt and pepper as needed

Instructions

1. The mixed salad greens, cherry tomatoes, cucumber slices, red onions, crumbled feta cheese, and chopped walnuts or almonds (if using) should all be mixed in a big bowl.
2. The balsamic vinaigrette combines the balsamic vinegar, extra virgin olive oil, Dijon mustard, honey or maple syrup, chopped garlic, salt, and pepper in a small bowl.
3. Drizzle the appropriate balsamic vinaigrette and gently mix to cover the salad's contents. If extra dressing is required, start with less and increase it as needed.
4. Add any extra toppings you like, such as sliced avocado, boiled eggs, or grilled chicken breast.
5. Enjoy the salad right away after serving it!

Nutrition information

Calories: 160 Carbohydrates: 10g Protein: 4g Fat: 12g Fiber: 2g Sugar: 5g

Beef and Vegetable Kebabs

Preparation time: 15 minutes

Marinating time: 30 minutes (optional)

Cooking time: 10-12 minutes

Ingredients

- 1 lb. beef sirloin, cut into 1-inch cubes
- 1 bell pepper, cut into 1-inch pieces
- 1 red onion, cut into 1-inch pieces
- 1 zucchini, cut into 1-inch thick slices
- 8-10 cherry tomatoes
- 2 tbsp olive oil
- 2 tbsp soy sauce
- 2 cloves garlic, minced

- 1 tsp paprika
- 1/2 tsp cumin
- Salt and pepper as need
- Optional garnish: Fresh parsley or cilantro

Instructions

1. The marinade is made by combining olive oil, soy sauce, minced garlic, paprika, cumin, salt, and pepper in a bowl.
2. Put the beef cubes in a different dish or a plastic bag that can be sealed. As you pour the marinade over the steak, ensure it is completely coated. Seal the plastic bag if you're using it, then slowly rub the marinade into the steak. Marinate in the refrigerator for at least 30 minutes or up to 2 hours.
3. Your grill or grill pan should be preheated over medium-high heat.
4. Cherry tomatoes, zucchini slices, bell pepper chunks, red onion chunks, and marinated beef cubes are alternately threaded onto skewers.
5. As the meat cooks to the appropriate doneness and the veggies become soft, grill the kebabs for 10 to 12 minutes, rotating once.
6. After removing the kebabs from the grill, give them some time to rest.
7. If preferred, garnish with fresh parsley or cilantro.
8. The Beef and Vegetable Kebabs should be served hot for a satisfying and protein-rich lunch.
9. Enjoy your tasty and flavorful kebabs!

Nutrition information (per serving, makes about 4 servings)

Calories: 320 Carbohydrates: 10g Protein: 25g Fat: 20g Fiber: 2g Sugar: 5g

Beef and Vegetable Stew with Beef Brisket

Preparation time: 15 minutes

Cooking time: 2.5 to 3 hours

Ingredients

- 2 lb. beef brisket, cut into 1-inch cubes
- 2 tbsp olive oil
- 1 large onion, diced
- 3 cloves garlic, minced
- 4 carrots, peeled and sliced
- 3 celery stalks, sliced
- 1 lb. potatoes, peeled and cut into chunks
- 1 can (14.5 oz.) diced tomatoes
- 4 cups of beef broth
- 2 tbsp tomato paste
- 1 tsp dried thyme
- 1 tsp dried rosemary
- Salt and pepper as need
- Optional garnish: Fresh parsley or thyme

Instructions

1. Warm the olive oil in a large pot or Dutch oven over medium-high heat.
2. Beef brisket cubes should be added to the saucepan and browned all over. The browned meat should be taken out of the saucepan and kept aside.
3. Add the minced garlic and onion to the same saucepan. The onion should be transparent after about 5 minutes of sautéing.

4. To the saucepan, add the diced potatoes, celery, and carrots. Cook for a further 3–4 minutes while stirring.
5. Bring back the beef brisket that has been browned. Add the beef broth, tomato paste, chopped tomatoes, dry thyme, and dried rosemary. As needed, add salt and pepper to the food.
6. When the mixture comes to a boil, turn the heat to low and cover the pan. Until the meat is tender and the flavors are well-balanced, simmer for 2.5 to 3 hours. Sometimes stir.
7. If necessary, taste and adjust the seasoning.
8. If preferred, top the steaming beef and vegetable stew bowls with fresh thyme or parsley.
9. Take pleasure in your warming and delicious Beef and Vegetable Stew!

Nutrition information

Calories: 420 Carbohydrates: 21g Protein: 35g Fat: 22g Fiber: 4g Sugar: 6g

Caribbean Grilled Pork

Preparation time: 15 minutes

Marinating time: 2 hours (or overnight for best flavor)

Grilling time: 15-20 minutes

Ingredients

- 2 lb. pork tenderloin
- 1/4 cup of orange juice
- 1/4 cup of lime juice
- 2 tbsp soy sauce
- 2 tbsp brown sugar
- 2 tbsp olive oil
- 2 cloves garlic, minced
- 1 tbsp ground allspice
- 1 tsp ground cinnamon
- 1 tsp ground ginger
- 1/2 tsp ground nutmeg
- 1/2 tsp ground black pepper
- Salt as need
- Optional garnish: Fresh chopped cilantro or green onions

Instructions

1. The marinade combines the orange juice, lime juice, soy sauce, brown sugar, olive oil, chopped garlic, ground ginger, ground nutmeg, black pepper, and salt in a bowl.
2. Put the pork tenderloin in a sealable plastic bag or a shallow plate. To ensure the meat is well covered, pour the marinade over it. Seal the plastic bag if you're using it, then massage the marinade into the pork. Marinate in the refrigerator for at least two hours or overnight for the finest taste.
3. Heat your grill to a moderately hot setting.
4. Take the pork tenderloin out of the marinade and throw away any extra.
5. Using a meat thermometer, grill the pork tenderloin for 15-20 minutes, turning it once or twice, or until it achieves an internal temperature of 145°F (63°C) for medium-rare or 160°F (71°C) for medium.
6. After the pork has finished cooking, take it off the grill and give it some time to rest.
7. Make thin slices of grilled pork.
8. If preferred, garnish with freshly cut cilantro or green onions.

9. Serving the Caribbean Grilled Pork hot is a tasty and savory main meal.
10. Enjoy your succulent and delicious Caribbean grilled pork!

Nutrition information

Calories: 300 Carbohydrates: 10g Protein: 30g Fat: 15g Fiber: 1g Sugar: 8g

Deep, Dark, and Stout Chili

Preparation time: 15 minutes

Cooking time: 1 hour 30 minutes

Ingredients

- 1.5 lb. ground beef or turkey
- 1 onion, diced
- 3 cloves garlic, minced
- 1 bell pepper, diced
- 2 cans (14.5 oz. every) diced tomatoes
- 1 can (15 oz.) tomato sauce
- 1 can (15 oz.) kidney beans, drained and rinsed
- 15 oz. black beans, drained and rinsed
- 1 cup of stout beer (such as Guinness)
- 2 tbsp tomato paste
- 2 tbsp chili powder
- 1 tbsp cocoa powder
- 1 tsp ground cumin
- 1 tsp smoked paprika
- 1/2 tsp dried oregano
- 1/2 tsp cayenne pepper (adjust to your spice preference)
- Salt and pepper as need

- Optional toppings: chopped green onions, Shredded cheddar cheese, sour cream

Instructions

1. Over medium heat, preheat a big saucepan or Dutch oven. Cooked the ground beef or turkey until browned after adding. If required, drain any extra fat.
2. Add the chopped bell pepper, onion, and garlic to the saucepan. To make the veggies soft, sauté for around 5 minutes.
3. The following ingredients should be added to the pot: diced tomatoes, tomato sauce, kidney beans, black beans, stout beer, tomato paste, chili powder, cocoa powder, ground cumin, smoked paprika, dried oregano, cayenne pepper, salt, and pepper. Mix everything well.
4. Once the chili has reached a rolling boil, turn down the heat. For one hour, boil the mixture under cover while stirring regularly to keep it from sticking.
5. After one hour, cover the pot and simmer for a further 30 minutes to thicken the chili and allow the flavors to blend. Periodically stir.
6. Taste the dish and, if necessary, add additional salt, pepper, or spices to the seasoning.
7. Top the Deep, Dark, and Stout Chili with sour cream, chopped green onions, and cheddar cheese shavings before serving.
8. Have a substantial, tasty bowl of Deep, Dark, and Stout Chili!

Nutrition information

Calories: 390 Carbohydrates: 32g Protein: 29g Fat: 14g Fiber: 10g Sugar: 7g

Grilled Shrimp Tacos

Preparation time: 15 minutes

Marinating time: 15 minutes (optional)

Cooking time: 6-8 minutes

Ingredients

- 1 lb. large shrimp, peeled and deveined
- 2 tbsp olive oil
- 2 cloves garlic, minced
- 1 tsp chili powder
- 1/2 tsp ground cumin
- 1/2 tsp paprika
- Salt and pepper as need
- 8 small flour or corn tortillas
- 1 cup of shredded cabbage or lettuce
- 1/2 cup of diced tomatoes
- 1/4 cup of diced red onion
- 1/4 cup of chopped fresh cilantro
- Lime wedges for serving

Instructions

1. Olive oil, minced garlic, chili powder, ground cumin, paprika, salt, and pepper should all be mixed in a bowl. When the shrimp are added, toss them until they are equally covered. If you have the time, let the shrimp marinate for 15 minutes.
2. Your grill or grill pan should be preheated over medium-high heat.
3. Throw the marinated shrimp onto skewers or use a grill basket for simple cooking.
4. The shrimp should be grilled on every side for two to three minutes until they are opaque and pink. Don't overcook them, please.
5. Once done, take the shrimp off the grill and place them elsewhere.
6. The tortillas should be warmed and made malleable by grilling them for 20 to 30 seconds on every side.
7. Place a tiny amount of finely chopped lettuce or cabbage on every tortilla before assembling the tacos. Add grilled shrimp, diced tomatoes, red onion, and fresh cilantro to the top.
8. For more flavor, squeeze some fresh lime juice over the tacos.
9. Enjoy the hot Grilled Shrimp Tacos after serving.

Nutrition information (per serving, based on 2 tacos)

Calories: 290 Carbohydrates: 27g Protein: 22g Fat: 10g Fiber: 4g Sugar: 3g

Chicken Salad Sandwich

Preparation time: 10 minutes

Cooking time: 0 minutes

Ingredients

- 2 cups of cooked chicken breast
- 1/2 cup of mayonnaise
- 2 tbsp Greek yogurt or sour cream
- 1 stalk celery, finely diced
- 1/4 cup of red onion
- 1/4 cup of chopped fresh parsley
- 1 tbsp Dijon mustard
- 1 tbsp lemon juice
- 1/2 tsp garlic powder
- Salt and pepper as need
- 8 slices of bread of your choice
- Lettuce leaves and tomato slices for sandwich assembly

Instructions

1. Cooked chicken breast, Greek yogurt or sour cream, celery and red onion sliced finely, fresh parsley cut finely, Dijon mustard, lemon juice, garlic powder, salt, and pepper should all be mixed in a bowl. All the components should be thoroughly mixed.
2. If necessary, taste and adjust the seasoning.
3. One slice of bread should be covered with the chicken salad mixture. The chicken salad with lettuce leaves and tomato slices.
4. Finish the sandwich by adding a second slice of bread.
5. To prepare more sandwiches, repeat the procedure.
6. If preferred, cut the sandwiches in half before serving.
7. Take pleasure in your fulfilling and delicious chicken salad sandwich!

Nutrition information

Calories: 450 Carbohydrates: 30g Protein: 27g Fat: 25g Fiber: 5g Sugar: 4g

Quinoa Bowls with Shrimp

Preparation time: 10 minutes

Cooking time: 20 minutes

Ingredients

- 1 cup of quinoa
- 1 lb. shrimp, peeled and deveined
- 2 tbsp olive oil, divided
- 1 tsp smoked paprika
- 1/2 tsp garlic powder
- Salt and pepper as need
- 1 bell pepper, diced
- 1 zucchini, diced
- 1 cup of cherry tomatoes, halved
- 1/4 cup of chopped fresh parsley
- Optional toppings: Avocado slices, lemon wedges

Instructions

1. Completely rinse the quinoa in cool water. The washed quinoa should be mixed with 2 cups of water in a medium pot. After boiling everything, turn down the heat and cover the pan. Stew the quinoa for 15 to 20 minutes or until it is fluffy and the water has been absorbed.
2. Take the shrimp in a bowl and season with salt, pepper, smoked paprika, garlic powder, and one tbsp of olive oil. Make sure the shrimp are covered evenly.
3. One more tbsp of olive oil is heated in a pan over medium heat. Add and fry the shrimp for two to three minutes on every side when the shrimp are pink and opaque. Don't overcook them, please. The shrimp should be taken out of the pan and put aside.
4. Add the chopped bell pepper and zucchini to the same skillet. They should be sautéed for 3 to 4 minutes until soft.
5. The cherry tomatoes should be slightly softened after being added to the pan and cooked for 2 minutes.
6. The cooked quinoa, sautéed veggies, and shrimp should all be mixed in a big dish. Gently mix everything by tossing.
7. Overtop the quinoa bowl, sprinkling chopped fresh parsley or cilantro.

8. Serve with lemon wedges on the side and, if wanted, avocado slices on top.
9. Enjoy your savory and nourishing shrimp and quinoa bowls!

Nutrition information

Calories: 370 Carbohydrates: 39g Protein: 27g Fat: 11g Fiber: 6g Sugar: 4g

Tomato with Garlicky Chives

Preparation time: 10 minutes

Cooking time: 10 minutes

Ingredients

- 4 large tomatoes
- 2 tbsp olive oil
- 2 cloves garlic, minced
- 2 tbsp chopped fresh chives
- Salt and pepper as need

Instructions

1. Turn on the oven to 400 °F.
2. The tomato shells should remain unbroken while you delicately remove the tops and scoop out the seeds and pulp. Tomato shells should be set aside.
3. Olive oil should be heated in a pan over medium heat. Add the minced garlic and cook until fragrant, about 1 to 2 minutes. Don't burn the garlic, please.
4. The chopped fresh chives should be added to the skillet and cooked for an additional one to two minutes or until they wilt gently.
5. After turning off the heat, let the mixture cool in the skillet.

6. Distribute the garlicky chive mixture equally among the tomato shells before stuffing them.
7. Season the filled tomatoes with salt and pepper on a baking sheet.
8. The tomatoes should be roasted through and soft after about 10 minutes in the preheated oven.
9. The tomatoes should be removed from the oven and given time to cool.
10. We warmly serve the Tomato with Garlicky Chives as a tasty and wholesome side dish or appetizer.
11. Enjoy the tasty fusion of garlicky chives and tomatoes!

Nutrition information (per serving, based on 1 tomato)

Calories: 80 Carbohydrates: 6g Protein: 2g Fat: 6g Fiber: 2g Sugar: 4g

Peppered Cheese with Stocky Cauliflower Soup

Preparation time: 15 minutes

Cooking time: 30 minutes

Ingredients

- 1 large head cauliflower, chopped into florets
- 1 onion, diced
- 2 cloves garlic, minced
- 4 cups of vegetable or chicken stock
- 1 cup of milk or plant-based milk
- 1 cup of shredded peppered cheese (such as pepper jack or peppered cheddar)
- 2 tbsp olive oil
- Salt and pepper as need

- Optional garnish: Chopped fresh parsley or chives

Instructions

1. Olive oil heated in a saucepan over medium heat. Add the minced garlic, onion, and sauté for approximately 5 minutes or until they are aromatic and transparent.
2. Add the chopped cauliflower florets to the saucepan, and cook for 3 to 4 minutes.
3. Cover the cauliflower and onions with the vegetable or chicken stock that has been added to the saucepan. Once the mixture boils, turn the heat low, cover, and simmer for 15-20 minutes or until the cauliflower is soft.
4. Blend the soup until it is smooth and creamy using a countertop mixer or an immersion blender. Hot liquids should be blended carefully since they can expand. When using a countertop blender, blend the mixture in small batches after letting it cool.
5. Put the soup back in the pot over low heat. Shredded peppered cheese and milk should be mixed well until the cheese has melted. As needed, add salt and pepper to the food.
6. Allow the flavors to blend by cooking the soup for 5 minutes.
7. Pour the stocky cauliflower soup into bowls and, if you'd like, top with chopped fresh chives or parsley.
8. Serving the peppered cheese with stocky cauliflower soup hot as a hearty and tasty supper.
9. Enjoy your rich and tasty soup.

Nutrition information

Calories: 250 Carbohydrates: 18g Protein: 11g Fat: 15g Fiber: 5g Sugar: 8g

Parsley Chickpea Bowls with Lemon

Preparation time: 15 minutes

Cooking time: 0 minutes

Ingredients

- 2 cups of cooked chickpeas
- 1 cup of chopped fresh parsley
- 1/2 cup of diced cucumber
- 1/2 cup of diced cherry tomatoes
- 1/4 cup of diced red onion
- Juice of 1 lemon
- 2 tbsp extra-virgin olive oil
- 1 clove garlic, minced
- Salt and pepper as need
- Optional toppings: Crumbled feta cheese, sliced avocado, toasted pine nuts

Instructions

1. The cooked chickpeas, fresh parsley cut, diced cucumber, cherry tomatoes, and red onion should all be mixed in a big bowl.
2. Mix the minced garlic, salt, lemon juice, extra virgin olive oil and pepper in a separate small bowl to make the dressing.
3. The chickpea mixture should be well-coated with the dressing after adding it.
4. If necessary, taste and adjust the seasoning.
5. Create dishes with the Parsley Chickpea combination.

6. Garnish the bowls with toasted pine nuts, feta cheese crumbles, and avocado slices if preferred.
7. Give your guests the Parsley Chickpea Bowls with Lemon for a light, healthy lunch.
8. Cheers to colorful and spicy chickpea bowls!

Nutrition information (per serving, based on 2 servings)

Calories: 370 Carbohydrates: 40g Protein: 12g Fat: 19g Fiber: 12g Sugar: 6g

Tomato with Cheesy Eggplant Sandwiches

Preparation time: 15 minutes

Cooking time: 15 minutes

Ingredients

- 1 large eggplant, sliced into 1/2-inch rounds
- 2 tbsp olive oil
- Salt and pepper as need
- 4 slices whole wheat bread
- 4 slices fresh mozzarella cheese
- 4 slices ripe tomato
- 1/4 cup of fresh basil leaves
- Optional spreads: Pesto, mayonnaise, or Dijon mustard

Instructions

1. Turn on the oven to 425 °F.
2. Brush olive oil on both sides of the eggplant slices before placing them on a baking pan. Add salt and pepper as need.
3. When the eggplant slices are soft and faintly browned, roast them in the preheated oven for 12-15 minutes, rotating them halfway through.
4. Slices of eggplant should be taken out of the oven and given some time to cool.
5. If preferred, toast the slices of whole wheat bread.
6. Spread pesto, mayonnaise, or Dijon mustard on one side of every slice of bread before assembling the sandwiches.
7. The spread over two slices of bread should be topped with a slice of fresh mozzarella cheese.
8. On top of the cheese, stack the roasted eggplant pieces.
9. Put a ripe tomato slice on top of the eggplant.
10. Top the tomato with a few basil leaves that are fresh.
11. To finish the sandwiches, place the remaining slices of bread on top.
12. If preferred, cut the sandwiches in half before serving.
13. Enjoy your tasty tomato-eggplant sandwiches!

Nutrition information (per sandwich, based on 1 sandwich)

Calories: 300 Carbohydrates: 27g Protein: 12g Fat: 17g Fiber: 8g Sugar: 6g

Lemony Salmon with Spicy Asparagus

Preparation time: 10 minutes

Cooking time: 15 minutes

Ingredients

- 2 salmon fillets (6-8 oz. every)

- 1 bunch asparagus, trimmed
- 2 tbsp olive oil
- Zest and juice of 1 lemon
- 1 tsp paprika
- 1/2 tsp cayenne pepper (adjust to your spice preference)
- Salt and pepper as need
- Optional garnish: Fresh chopped parsley

Instructions

1. Turn on the oven to 400 °F.
2. Arrange the salmon fillets on a baking sheet covered with aluminium foil or parchment paper. Add lemon zest, salt, and pepper to the salmon, along with 1 tbsp of olive oil.
3. Mix the lemon juice, paprika, cayenne, and 1 tbsp of olive oil in a small bowl.
4. To uniformly coat the salmon fillets, brush on the lemon-spice mixture.
5. Place the salmon fillets and the trimmed asparagus stalks on the same baking sheet. Salt and pepper them, then drizzle a little olive oil over them.
6. When the salmon is cooked through and flakes easily with a fork, place the baking sheet in the preheated oven and bake for 12-15 minutes. Depending on the thickness of the salmon fillets, the cooking time may change.
7. The salmon and asparagus should rest for a few minutes after the baking sheet has been taken out of the oven.
8. Garnish the hot, Lemony Salmon and Spicy Asparagus with freshly chopped parsley if preferred.
9. Enjoy your tasty and filling dinner!

Nutrition information (per serving, based on 2 servings)

Calories: 420 Carbohydrates: 9g Protein: 34g Fat: 28g Fiber: 4g Sugar: 4g

Halibut with Lime and Ginger

Cooking time: 12 minutes

Preparation time: 15 minutes

Ingredients

- 4 halibut fillets (about 6 oz. every)
- 2 tbsp fresh lime juice
- 1 tbsp grated fresh ginger
- 2 cloves garlic, minced
- 2 tbsp soy sauce
- 1 tbsp honey
- 1 tbsp sesame oil
- Salt and pepper as need
- Fresh cilantro, chopped (for garnish)

Instructions

1. Turn on the oven to 400 °F. Used parchment paper to line a baking sheet or gently oil it.
2. Mix the lime juice, minced garlic, ginger, soy sauce, honey, sesame oil, salt, and pepper in a small bowl.
3. Halibut fillets should be placed on the prepared baking sheet. Ensure the fillets are properly coated before adding the lime and ginger mixture. For approximately ten minutes, let them marinade.
4. Take the baking sheet in the preheated oven after marinating. Halibut should be baked for 12

minutes or until it flakes easily and is well-cooked.

5. Halibut should be taken out of the oven and given time to rest. This will enable the flavors to converge and the fish to gradually firm up.

6. With the remaining marinade poured on top, serve the halibut fillets. Add freshly chopped cilantro as a garnish.

Nutritional information (per serving)

Calories: 250 Protein: 36g Fat: 8g Carbohydrates: 7g Fiber: 0.5g

Lentils and Rice

Cooking time: 30 minutes

Preparation time: 10 minutes

Ingredients

- 1 cup of dried lentils
- 1 cup of basmati rice
- 2 tbsp olive oil
- 1 onion, finely chopped
- 2 cloves garlic, minced
- 1 tsp cumin
- 1 tsp turmeric
- 1 tsp paprika
- 4 cups of vegetable broth
- Salt and pepper as need
- Fresh parsley, chopped (for garnish)

Instructions

1. Put the lentils aside after giving them a cold water rinse. Rinse the rice in another bowl until the water is clear, then put it aside.

2. Olive oil heated in a saucepan over medium heat. Add the minced garlic, onion, and sauté until they are aromatic and transparent.

3. Stir well to evenly distribute the cumin, turmeric, and paprika throughout the pot's onions and garlic.

4. After washing, lentils, rice, and vegetable broth should all be added to the pot. As needed, add salt and pepper to the food.

5. When the mixture boils, turn the heat low and cover the pan. Allow it to simmer for around 20 minutes or until the rice and lentils are cooked and soaked up most of the liquid.

6. Once the food is prepared, please turn off the heat and let it rest, covered, for a few minutes to absorb any moisture.

7. Rice and lentils should be fluffed with a fork. If necessary, taste and adjust the seasoning.

8. Hot lentils and rice should be served with freshly chopped parsley on top.

9. Enjoy your filling rice and lentils meal!

Nutritional information (per serving)

Calories: 350 Protein: 15g Fat: 8g Carbohydrates: 57g Fiber: 14g

Cannellini Bean Pizza

Cooking time: 15-20 minutes

Preparation time: 15 minutes

Ingredients

- 1 pre-made pizza dough (store-bought or homemade)
- 1 can (15 oz.) cannellini beans, drained and rinsed
- 2 tbsp olive oil
- 2 cloves garlic, minced
- 1 tsp dried oregano
- 1 cup of shredded mozzarella cheese
- 1 cup of cherry tomatoes, halved
- Handful of fresh basil leaves, torn
- Salt and pepper as need

Instructions

1. Pre-heat your oven to the temperature recommended on the pizza dough packaging, often 425°F (220°C).
2. Cannellini beans, olive oil, minced garlic, dried oregano, salt, and pepper should all be mixed in a food processor. Until smooth, process the beans to make a creamy bean spread.
3. The pizza dough should be rolled out to the required thickness on a lightly dusted surface. Take the dough on a pizza stone or baking sheet.
4. Leave a thin border around the borders and cover the pizza dough with the cannellini bean mixture equally.
5. Over the bean mixture, strew mozzarella cheese crumbles.
6. Place the cheese on top of the cherry tomatoes, cut in half. As needed, add salt and pepper to the food.
7. In a preheated oven, pizza should be baked for 15-20 minutes or until the dough is golden brown and the cheese is melted and bubbling.
8. Pizza should be taken out of the oven and given some time to cool. Add some chopped fresh basil on top.
9. Pizza should be sliced and served hot.
10. Eat your delicious pizza made with cannellini beans!

Nutritional information (per serving)

Calories: 280 Protein: 11g Fat: 11g Carbohydrates: 35g Fiber: 5g

Garbanzo Bean Curry

Cooking time: 30 minutes

Preparation time: 15 minutes

Ingredients

- 2 tbsp vegetable oil
- 1 onion, finely chopped
- 3 cloves garlic, minced
- 1 tbsp fresh ginger, grated
- 1 tbsp curry powder
- 1 tsp ground cumin
- 1 tsp ground coriander
- 1/2 tsp turmeric
- 1/4 tsp cayenne pepper (adjust as needed)
- 1 can garbanzo beans, drained and rinsed
- 1 can (14 oz.) diced tomatoes
- 1 cup of coconut milk
- Salt as need

- Fresh cilantro, chopped (for garnish)

Instructions

1. Warm the vegetable oil in a large skillet or saucepan set over medium heat. The chopped onion should be added and cooked until soft and transparent.
2. Grated ginger and minced garlic should be added to the skillet. Saute until aromatic for one more minute.
3. Curry powder, ground cumin, coriander, turmeric, and cayenne pepper should all be mixed in a small bowl. As the onion, garlic, and ginger are coated, stir the spice mixture into the pan.
4. Diced tomatoes and the drained and washed garbanzo beans should be added to the pan. To thoroughly incorporate all the ingredients, stir well.
5. Add the coconut milk, then mix once more. As needed, add salt to the dish.
6. For approximately 15 to 20 minutes, bring the mixture to a simmer and let it cook so the flavors mingle and the sauce thickens.
7. Take the skillet from the stove. Use freshly cut cilantro as a garnish for the garbanzo bean curry.
8. With naan bread or steaming rice, serve the curry hot.
9. Enjoy your tasty curry made with garbanzo beans!

Nutritional information (per serving)

Calories: 320 Protein: 10g Fat: 15g Carbohydrates: 40g Fiber: 10g

Potato Salad

Cooking time: 15 minutes

Preparation time: 15 minutes

Ingredients

- 2 lb. potatoes (Yukon Gold or red potatoes work well)
- 1/2 cup of mayonnaise
- 2 tbsp Dijon mustard
- 2 tbsp white vinegar
- 1/2 cup of diced celery
- 1/4 cup of diced red onion
- 1/4 cup of chopped dill pickles
- 2 hard-boiled eggs, chopped
- Salt and pepper as need
- Fresh parsley, chopped (for garnish)

Instructions

1. Put the potatoes in a big saucepan and add water to cover them. Over high heat, bring the water to a rolling boil. Reduced the heat to medium when the potatoes are fork-tender, and simmer them for 10 to 15 minutes.
2. The potatoes should be drained and let to cool somewhat. Peel the potatoes and then chop them into bite-sized pieces once they are cold enough to handle.
3. Mayonnaise, Dijon mustard, white vinegar, salt, and pepper should all be well mixed in a big basin.
4. Add the diced celery, red onion, chopped dill pickles, and chopped hard-boiled eggs to the bowl containing the dressing. Gently blend by stirring.
5. Cubed potatoes should be added to the bowl and gently mixed with the

remaining ingredients and dressing until thoroughly mixed.

6. Test the potato salad and add more salt and pepper if necessary to adjust the flavor.
7. Before serving, chill the potato salad for at least an hour in the fridge. This will enable the flavors to converge.
8. Garnish the potato salad with freshly cut parsley right before serving.
9. Enjoy your potato salad, which is wonderful and creamy.

Nutritional information (per serving)

Calories: 300 Protein: 6g Fat: 17g Carbohydrates: 33g Fiber: 4g

Spinach Berry Salad

Preparation time: 15 minutes

Ingredients

- 6 cups of baby spinach leaves
- 1 cup of strawberries, hulled and sliced
- 1 cup of blueberries
- 1/2 cup of raspberries
- 1/4 cup of sliced almonds
- 1/4 cup of crumbled feta cheese
- 2 tbsp balsamic vinegar
- 1 tbsp honey
- 2 tbsp extra-virgin olive oil
- Salt and pepper as need

Instructions

1. Baby spinach, strawberries, blueberries, raspberries, sliced almonds, and crumbled feta cheese

should all be mixed in a large salad dish.

2. Balsamic vinegar, honey, extra virgin olive oil, salt, and pepper should all be well blended in a small bowl.
3. Toss the salad carefully to distribute the dressing over all ingredients evenly.
4. The spinach berry salad should be served right away.
5. Take pleasure in your healthy and hydrating spinach berry salad.

Nutritional information (per serving)

Calories: 180 Protein: 5g Fat: 11g Carbohydrates: 18g Fiber: 5g

Healthy Minestrone Soup

Cooking time: 30 minutes

Preparation time: 15 minutes

Ingredients

- 2 tbsp olive oil
- 1 onion, diced
- 2 cloves garlic, minced
- 2 carrots, diced
- 2 celery stalks, diced
- 1 zucchini, diced
- 1 cup of green beans
- 1 can (14 oz.) diced tomatoes
- 4 cups of vegetable broth
- 2 cups of water
- 1 cup of small pasta (such as shells or elbows)
- 1 can (15 oz.) cannellini beans, drained and rinsed
- 1 tsp dried oregano
- 1 tsp dried basil

- Salt and pepper as need
- Fresh parsley, chopped (for garnish)

Instructions

1. Warm the olive oil over medium heat in a large saucepan or Dutch oven. Garlic and onion, both diced, should be added and sautéed until aromatic.
2. Add chopped carrots, celery, zucchini, and green beans to the saucepan. The veggies should start to soften after a few minutes of sautéing.
3. Mix in the water, vegetable broth, and chopped tomatoes. The mixture is brought to a boil.
4. Small pasta should be added to the saucepan and cooked according to the package directions until al dente.
5. Stir in the cannellini beans, dried oregano, dry basil, salt, and pepper when the pasta has finished cooking. To allow the flavors to mingle, simmer for a further 5–10 minutes.
6. If necessary, check the soup's flavor and season as needed.
7. Fill dishes with the minestrone soup and top with freshly cut parsley.
8. Enjoy the soup when it is served hot!

Nutritional information (per serving)

Calories: 250 Protein: 10g Fat: 6g
Carbohydrates: 40g Fiber: 8g

Quinoa Vegetable Soup

Cooking time: 30 minutes

Preparation time: 15 minutes

Ingredients

- 1 tbsp olive oil
- 1 onion, diced
- 2 cloves garlic, minced
- 2 carrots, diced
- 2 celery stalks, diced
- 1 zucchini, diced
- 1 bell pepper, diced
- 1 can (14 oz.) diced tomatoes
- 6 cups of vegetable broth
- 1 cup of quinoa, rinsed
- 1 tsp dried thyme
- 1 tsp dried oregano
- Salt and pepper as need
- Fresh parsley, chopped (for garnish)

Instructions

1. Warm olive oil in a large pot or Dutch oven over medium-high heat. Add the minced garlic and onion, and cook them together until they are aromatic and tender.
2. The saucepan should now contain the chopped carrots, celery, zucchini, and bell pepper. Vegetables should be sautéed for a few minutes until they start to soften.
3. Add salt, pepper, dried thyme, dry oregano, vegetable broth, rinsed quinoa, and chopped tomatoes after stirring. The mixture should boil.
4. Once the quinoa and carrots are soft, boil the heat to low and let the soup simmer for about 20 minutes.

5. If necessary, taste the soup and adjust the seasoning.
6. Fill bowls with the quinoa veggie soup and top with freshly chopped parsley.
7. Enjoy the soup while it's still hot!

Nutritional information (per serving)

Calories: 280 Protein: 10g Fat: 5g Carbohydrates: 52g Fiber: 8g

German Potato Soup

Cooking time: 40 minutes

Preparation time: 15 minutes

Ingredients

- 4 slices bacon, chopped
- 1 onion, diced
- 2 cloves garlic, minced
- 4 cups of chicken or vegetable broth
- 1 ½ lb. potatoes, peeled and diced
- 2 carrots, diced
- 2 celery stalks, diced
- 1 tsp dried thyme
- 1 bay leaf
- Salt and pepper as needed
- ½ cup of heavy cream (optional)
- Fresh chives, chopped (for garnish)

Instructions

1. Cook the diced bacon to crispiness in a large soup pot over medium heat. While keeping the rendered fat in the saucepan, remove the bacon and set it aside.
2. Add the minced garlic and onion to the bacon fat-containing saucepan. The onion should be sautéed until tender and transparent.

3. Add the chopped potatoes, carrots, celery, dried thyme, bay leaf, salt, and pepper to the saucepan, then the chicken or vegetable stock. To blend, thoroughly stir.
4. When the potatoes and veggies are cooked, simmer the mixture for 25 to 30 minutes after bringing it to a boil.
5. From the soup, remove the bay leaf. Partially purée the soup using a potato masher or immersion blender to give it a creamy texture while retaining some potato and vegetable bits.
6. If you want to give the soup more richness, whisk in some heavy cream. For a few more minutes, gently reheat the soup.
7. German potato soup should be poured into bowls. Add the crispy bacon bits and freshly cut chives as garnish.
8. Enjoy the soup while it's still hot!

Nutritional information (per serving)

Calories: 280 Protein: 8g Fat: 15g Carbohydrates: 30g Fiber: 4g

Pasta Primavera

Cooking time: 15 minutes

Preparation time: 15 minutes

Ingredients

- 8 oz. pasta (linguine or fettuccine work well)
- 2 tbsp olive oil
- 2 cloves garlic, minced
- 1 small onion, thinly sliced
- 1 carrot, julienned

- 1 bell pepper, thinly sliced
- 1 small zucchini, thinly sliced
- 1 cup of broccoli florets
- 1 cup of cherry tomatoes, halved
- 1/2 cup of vegetable broth
- 1/4 cup of grated Parmesan cheese
- 2 tbsp chopped fresh basil
- Salt and pepper as needed

Instructions

1. Follow package directions to cook pasta al dente. Drain and reserve.
2. Melt the olive oil in a large pan over medium heat. Mix the onion slices and garlic powder. Sauté the onion until it softens and turns translucent.
3. Add the broccoli florets, thinly sliced bell pepper, julienned carrot, and thinly sliced zucchini to the pan. The veggies should be crisp-tender after a short time in the sauté pan.
4. Add the halved cherry tomatoes and vegetable broth after stirring. Until the tomatoes soften, cook for a further 2 to 3 minutes.
5. Toss the veggies and cooked pasta together in the skillet. Allow the flavors to blend by cooking for a few minutes.
6. Take the skillet off the heat. Add the chopped fresh basil and Parmesan cheese after stirring. Add pepper and salt as needed when seasoning.
7. Top the hot pasta primavera with more Parmesan cheese and fresh basil if preferred.
8. Enjoy your colorful and tasty pasta!

Nutritional information (per serving)

Calories: 320 Protein: 10g Fat: 10g
Carbohydrates: 50g Fiber: 5g

CHAPTER 3: DINNER RECIPES

Smoky Hawaiian Pork

Cooking time: 3 hours

Preparation time: 15 minutes

Ingredients

- 2 lb. pork shoulder, cut into chunks
- 1 tbsp smoked paprika
- 1 tsp garlic powder
- 1 tsp onion powder
- 1 tsp ground cumin
- 1 tsp ground coriander
- 1/2 tsp cayenne pepper (adjust as needed)
- 1/4 cup of low-sodium soy sauce
- 1/4 cup of pineapple juice
- 2 tbsp brown sugar
- 2 tbsp apple cider vinegar
- 1 tbsp vegetable oil
- 1 cup of pineapple chunks
- Salt and pepper as needed
- Fresh cilantro, chopped (for garnish)

Instructions

1. Set your oven's temperature to 325 °F (165 °C).
2. The smoked paprika, garlic powder, onion powder, ground cumin, ground coriander, and cayenne pepper should all be mixed in a small bowl. After seasoning the pork shoulder pieces with salt and pepper, sprinkle them evenly with

the spice mixture and massage them.

3. Vegetable oil should be heated in a large Dutch oven or oven-safe saucepan over medium-high heat. Add the seasoned pork shoulder pieces and fry them for 2 to 3 minutes every side or until they are browned on both sides.

4. Low-sodium soy sauce, pineapple juice, brown sugar, and apple cider vinegar should all be mixed in a different bowl. Over the seared pork shoulder in the saucepan, pour this mixture.

5. Distribute the pineapple pieces around the pork shoulder in the pot.

6. Put a cover on the saucepan and place it in the preheated oven. When the pork is soft and readily shredded with a fork, cook for about 2 1/2 to 3 hours.

7. After cooking, take the saucepan out of the oven. Shred the pork shoulder into smaller pieces using two forks.

8. Serve the Smoky Hawaiian Pork hot with fresh cilantro that has been chopped.

Nutritional information (per serving)

Calories: 350 Protein: 32g Fat: 20g Carbohydrates: 11g Fiber: 1g

Chipotle Tacos

Cooking time: 20 minutes

Preparation time: 10 minutes

Ingredients

- 1 lb. chicken breasts, boneless and skinless
- 2 tbsp olive oil
- 2 chipotle peppers in adobo sauce, minced
- 2 cloves garlic, minced
- 1 tsp ground cumin
- 1 tsp chilli powder
- 1/2 tsp smoked paprika
- Salt and pepper as needed
- 8 small corn tortillas
- Toppings: diced tomatoes, shredded lettuce, chopped cilantro, sliced avocado, sour cream, lime wedges, etc. (optional)

Instructions

1. Minced chipotle peppers, minced garlic, ground cumin, chilli powder, smoked paprika, salt, and pepper should all be mixed in a bowl. Mix thoroughly.

2. Do so as you uniformly coat the chicken breasts with the spice mixture.

3. Olive oil heated to a medium-high temperature in a skillet. The seasoned chicken breasts should be added to the skillet and cooked on every side for 6 to 8 minutes until done and no longer pink in the middle. Take it off the stove and give it some time to cool.

4. Warm the corn tortillas while the chicken is resting. They can be softened by heating them briefly in the microwave or for approximately

30 seconds per side in a dry pan over medium heat.

5. Cooked chicken breasts should be sliced into thin strips.

6. Sliced chipotle chicken should be placed into every corn tortilla. Add the toppings of your choice, such as diced tomatoes, lettuce, cilantro, avocado slices, sour cream, and a squeeze of lime juice.

7. Warm Chipotle tacos should be served.

8. Enjoy your hot and tasty Chipotle tacos!

Nutritional information (per serving, without toppings)

Calories: 250 Protein: 25g Fat: 9g
Carbohydrates: 15g Fiber: 2g

Zesty Pepper Beef

Cooking time: 15 minutes

Preparation time: 10 minutes

Ingredients

- 1 lb. beef sirloin, thinly sliced
- 2 tbsp soy sauce
- 2 tbsp Worcestershire sauce
- 2 tbsp balsamic vinegar
- 2 cloves garlic, minced
- 1 tsp paprika
- 1/2 tsp red pepper flakes (adjust as needed)
- 1/2 tsp black pepper
- 2 tbsp vegetable oil
- 1 green bell pepper, sliced
- 1 red bell pepper, sliced
- 1 yellow bell pepper, sliced
- 1 onion, thinly sliced
- Salt as need

- Fresh parsley, chopped (for garnish)

Instructions

1. The soy sauce, Worcestershire sauce, paprika, balsamic vinegar, minced garlic, red pepper flakes, and black pepper should all be mixed in a bowl. Mix thoroughly.

2. Put the beef sirloin that has been thinly cut in the basin with the marinade. Toss to coat the meat evenly. Give it about 10 minutes to marinate.

3. Heat the vegetable oil over medium-high heat in a big skillet or wok. When the meat is browned and cooked to your preferred doneness, add the marinated steak and stir-fry for about 2-3 minutes. Please remove the meat from the skillet and set it aside.

4. Add the onion and bell pepper slices to the same skillet. 3–4 minutes of stirring should be sufficient to achieve tender-crispness.

5. The peppers, onions, and cooked meat should all be added to the pan. As needed, add salt to the dish. Stir-fry for one more minute to fully reheat and meld the flavors.

6. Take the skillet from the stove. Add freshly cut parsley as a garnish to the Zesty Pepper Beef.

7. Serve the Zesty Pepper Beef hot with rice or noodles or as a stand-alone meal.

8. Enjoy your tasty and spicy Zesty Pepper Beef!

Nutritional information (per serving)

Calories: 280 Protein: 26g Fat: 16g
Carbohydrates: 10g Fiber: 3g

Warm Barley Salad with Spring Veggies

Cooking time: 40 minutes

Preparation time: 15 minutes

Ingredients

- 1 cup of pearl barley
- 2 cups of vegetable broth
- 1 tbsp olive oil
- 1 small onion, diced
- 2 cloves garlic, minced
- 1 cup of asparagus, cut into 1-inch pieces
- 1 cup of sugar snap peas, ends trimmed and halved
- 1 cup of cherry tomatoes, halved
- 1 tbsp fresh lemon juice
- 2 tbsp chopped fresh parsley
- Salt and pepper as needed
- Crumbled feta cheese (optional for garnish)

Instructions

1. Put the pearl barley through a cold water rinse. Barley that has been washed and vegetable broth should be mixed. Bring to a boil, lower the heat to a simmer, cover the pot, and cook for 30 -35 minutes, or until the barley is cooked through and has absorbed the liquid. Barley has been cooked; drain any extra liquid, and set aside.
2. Olive oil should be heated in a large pan over medium heat. Add the minced garlic and onion, and cook until the onion is transparent and tender.
3. The skillet should now include the asparagus and sugar snap peas. Cook vegetables until crisp-tender, 3–4 minutes.
4. Cooked barley and cherry tomatoes are added, and the mixture is heated for 1-2 minutes.
5. Take the skillet from the stove. Fresh lemon juice drizzled over the heated barley and veggies. Add freshly cut parsley, then season with salt and pepper to suit.
6. Toss the ingredients together carefully.
7. Warm up the Warm Barley Salad and Spring Veggies before serving. Feta cheese crumbles can be used as a garnish if preferred for flavor.

Nutritional information (per serving)

Calories: 280 Protein: 9g Fat: 5g
Carbohydrates: 54g Fiber: 10g

Roasted Shrimp and Veggies Recipe

Preparation Time: 15 minutes

Cooking Time: 20 minutes

Total Time: 35 minutes

Ingredients

- 1 lb. large shrimp, peeled and deveined
- 2 medium zucchini, sliced
- 1 red bell pepper, sliced
- 1 yellow bell pepper, sliced
- 1 red onion, sliced

- 2 cloves garlic, minced
- 3 tbsp olive oil
- 1 tsp dried thyme
- 1 tsp dried oregano
- 1/2 tsp paprika
- Salt and black pepper as needed
- Fresh parsley, chopped (for garnish)

Instructions

1. Put a baking sheet in the oven and preheat it to 425 °F (220 °C).
2. Mix the shrimp with the sliced zucchini, bell peppers, red onion, minced garlic, olive oil, dried thyme, dried oregano, paprika, salt, and black pepper in a large bowl. Mix everything and toss until the shrimp and veggies are uniformly seasoned.
3. On the baking sheet that has been prepared, spread the shrimp and vegetable mixture in a single layer.
4. Stirring once midway through cooking, roast in the oven for about 15-20 minutes or until the shrimp is cooked through and the veggies are soft.
5. Take the baking sheet from the oven and sprinkle with fresh parsley.
6. As a main meal or over a bed of rice, quinoa, or pasta, serve the hot, roasted shrimp and vegetables.

Nutrition Information (per serving)

Calories: 260 Protein: 23g Fat: 11g
Carbohydrates: 18g Fiber: 5g

Shrimp and Pineapple Lettuce Wraps

Preparation Time: 20 minutes

Cooking Time: 10 minutes

Total Time: 30 minutes

Ingredients

- 1 lb. large shrimp, peeled and deveined
- 1 cup of fresh pineapple, diced
- 1 red bell pepper, diced
- 1/2 cup of shredded carrots
- 4 green onions, chopped
- 2 cloves garlic, minced
- 2 tbsp soy sauce (or tamari for gluten-free)
- 1 tbsp honey or maple syrup
- 1 tbsp lime juice
- 1 tbsp sesame oil
- 1/2 tsp grated ginger
- Salt and black pepper as needed
- Lettuce leaves (such as butter lettuce or iceberg) for wrapping
- Optional toppings: chopped cilantro, chopped peanuts, lime wedges

Instructions

1. Mix the soy sauce, honey or maple syrup, lime juice, sesame oil, chopped ginger, salt, and black pepper in a small bowl. Set apart.
2. Over medium-high heat, preheat a large skillet or wok. The shrimp should be cooked in the skillet for two to three minutes on every side or until they turn pink and opaque. Take the shrimp out of the skillet and place them aside.

3. The bell pepper, carrots, and green onions should all be added to the same pan. Until somewhat softened, sauté for 2 to 3 minutes.
4. Add the pineapple to the pan and cook for 1-2 minutes when it is fully heated.
5. Put the cooked shrimp back in the skillet with the prepared sauce, then top with the veggies. All of the ingredients should be well covered after being stirred. To let the flavors mix, cook for one to two more minutes.
6. After taking the skillet from the heat, let the mixture gradually cool.
7. When it's time to serve, put the shrimp and pineapple mixture onto every lettuce leaf, roll them up, and, if you like, fasten them with toothpicks.
8. Serve with lime wedges and optional garnishes like cilantro and peanuts that have been chopped.

Nutrition Information (per serving, excluding optional toppings)

Calories: 220 Protein: 25g Fat: 4g Carbohydrates: 22g Fiber: 4g

Grilled Scallops with Gremolata

Preparation Time: 15 minutes

Marinating Time: 30 minutes

Cooking Time: 6-8 minutes

Total Time: 51-53 minutes

Ingredients

- 1 lb. scallops

- 2 tbsp olive oil
- 2 cloves garlic, minced
- Zest of 1 lemon
- 2 tbsp fresh parsley, finely chopped
- Salt and black pepper as needed
- Lemon wedges for serving

Instructions

1. The gremolata marinade combines olive oil, minced garlic, lemon zest, chopped parsley, salt, and black pepper in a small bowl.
2. Put the scallops in a small dish and cover them with the gremolata marinade. Toss to coat the scallops evenly. For about 30 minutes, cover the dish and marinate the scallops in the fridge.
3. Set the grill's temperature to medium-high.
4. Scallops should be removed from the marinade, letting any extra marinade drop off.
5. Be cautious not to overcook the scallops, as they should only be fried on every side for two to three minutes. The size of the scallops will determine the precise cooking time.
6. When the scallops are done, take them off the grill and place them on a serving plate.
7. Serve the hot, grilled scallops with extra parsley that has been minced and lemon wedges on the side.

Nutrition Information (per serving)

Calories: 200 Protein: 20g Fat: 9g Carbohydrates: 3g Fiber: 0g

Healthy Paella

Preparation Time: 15 minutes

Cooking Time: 45 minutes

Total Time: 60 minutes

Ingredients

- 1 tbsp olive oil
- 1 onion, diced
- 2 cloves garlic, minced
- 1 red bell pepper, diced
- 1 yellow bell pepper, diced
- 1 cup of diced tomatoes
- 1 cup of Arborio or short-grain rice
- 2 cups of low-sodium vegetable broth
- 1 tsp smoked paprika
- 1/2 tsp turmeric
- 1/2 tsp saffron threads (optional)
- 1/2 tsp dried thyme
- 1/2 tsp dried oregano
- Salt and black pepper as needed
- 1 cup of frozen peas
- 1 cup of cooked chicken breast, diced
- 1/2 lb. shrimp, peeled and deveined
- 1/2 lb. mussels or clams, cleaned
- Fresh parsley, chopped (for garnish)
- Lemon wedges (for serving)

Instructions

1. Heat the olive oil in a large paella pan or skillet over medium heat. Add the minced garlic and onion, and cook for two to three minutes or until soft.
2. Diced red and yellow bell peppers should be added to the skillet and cooked for a further 2-3 minutes or until they soften.
3. The chopped tomatoes should release their juices after 2 minutes of cooking after being stirred in.
4. Rice should be added to the pan and mixed with the veggie mixture.
5. The vegetable broth should be warmed to a low simmer in a separate saucepan. Add the smoked paprika, turmeric, salt, black pepper, dried thyme, dried oregano, and saffron threads (if using). Pour the flavorful broth over the rice and veggies in the pan. Stir everything well.
6. Turn down the heat to low and put a lid on the pan. The rice should be virtually cooked after 20 minutes of simmering the paella.
7. Over the rice, distribute the frozen peas, chopped chicken breast, shrimp, and mussels or clams. Once again, covering the pan, simmer the seafood for an additional 10-15 minutes or until it is well cooked, and the mussels or clams have opened.
8. When the paella is finished, turn off the heat and give it some time to cool.
9. Serve hot, topped with parsley and lemon wedges.

Nutrition Information (per serving)

Calories: 350 Protein: 25g Fat: 5g
Carbohydrates: 50g Fiber: 4g

Baked Pork Chops

Preparation Time: 10 minutes

Cooking Time: 25 minutes

Total Time: 35 minutes

Ingredients

- 4 boneless pork chops
- 2 tbsp olive oil
- 1 tsp garlic powder
- 1 tsp paprika
- 1/2 tsp dried thyme
- 1/2 tsp dried rosemary
- Salt and black pepper as needed
- Optional: Fresh herbs (such as parsley or thyme) for garnish

Instructions

1. A baking sheet should be lined with aluminium foil while your oven is preheated to 400°F (200°C).
2. Paint the pork chops dry using paper towels to remove any extra moisture.
3. Mix the garlic powder, paprika, dried thyme, rosemary, salt, and black pepper in a small bowl.
4. The pork chops should have olive oil applied to both sides.
5. Sprinkle the seasoning evenly over the pork chops' top and bottom surfaces, then massage it to help it stick.
6. On the baking sheet that has been prepared, put the seasoned pork chops.
7. After 20–25 minutes in the preheated oven, pork chops should be medium-done at 145°F (63°C). The thickness of the pork chops will affect how long they need to cook.

8. After cooking, take the pork chops out of the oven and give them some time to rest.
9. If preferred, top the hot baked pork chops with fresh herbs before serving.

Nutrition Information (per serving, based on 1 pork chop)

Calories: 250 Protein: 30g Fat: 14g
Carbohydrates: 1g Fiber: 0g

Shish Kabob

Preparation Time: 20 minutes

Marinating Time: 1-2 hours (optional)

Cooking Time: 10-15 minutes

Total Time: 1 hour 30 minutes

Ingredients

- 1 lb. beef (such as sirloin or tenderloin), cut into 1-inch cubes
- 1 lb. chicken breast, cut into 1-inch cubes
- 1 red bell pepper, cut into chunks
- 1 green bell pepper, cut into chunks
- 1 yellow bell pepper, cut into chunks
- 1 red onion, cut into chunks
- 8-10 cherry tomatoes
- 8-10 button mushrooms
- 2 tbsp olive oil
- 2 tbsp lemon juice
- 2 cloves garlic, minced
- 1 tsp dried oregano
- 1 tsp dried thyme
- 1 tsp paprika
- Salt and black pepper as needed
- Metal or bamboo skewers

Instructions

1. Mix the olive oil, lemon juice, minced garlic, dried thyme, dried oregano, paprika, salt, and black pepper in a big bowl to make the marinade.
2. Chicken and beef cubes should be added to the marinade, and they should be well-coated. To improve the flavor, cover the bowl and place the meat in the refrigerator for at least one to two hours. You can move on to the following step without marinating the meat if pressed for time.
3. Heat your grill to a moderately hot setting.
4. On the skewers, alternately thread the marinated meat, chicken, bell pepper, onion pieces, cherry tomatoes, and mushrooms.
5. When the meat is cooked to your preferred doneness, and the veggies are soft, place the skewers on the prepared grill and cook for about 10-15 minutes, flipping once or twice.
6. Once done, take the skewers from the grill and give them a moment to rest.
7. Serve the shish kabobs hot with rice, salad, or pita bread as a side dish.

Nutrition Information (per serving, based on 1 skewer)

Calories: 250 Protein: 25g Fat: 10g
Carbohydrates: 12g Fiber: 3g

Barbecued Chicken

Preparation Time: 15 minutes

Marinating Time: 1-4 hours

Cooking Time: 30-40 minutes

Ingredients

- 4 chicken leg quarters (or a combination of chicken drumsticks and thighs)
- 1 cup of barbecue sauce (your favourite brand or homemade)
- 2 tbsp olive oil
- 2 tbsp apple cider vinegar
- 2 tbsp honey or brown sugar
- 2 cloves garlic, minced
- 1 tsp smoked paprika
- 1/2 tsp chilli powder
- 1/2 tsp onion powder
- Salt and black pepper as needed

Instructions

1. Barbecue sauce, olive oil, apple cider vinegar, honey or brown sugar, garlic powder, smoked paprika, chilli powder, onion powder, salt, and black pepper should all be mixed in a bowl. To prepare the marinade, whisk everything together.
2. The chicken leg parts should be put in a large zip-top bag or shallow plate. To ensure the chicken is well covered, pour the marinade over it. Refrigerate for 1-4 hours to let the tastes meld, then seal the bag or cover the dish. If you're short on time, marinate for 30 minutes.
3. Heat your grill to a moderately hot setting.

4. Take the chicken out of the marinade and save the extra for basting.

5. The skin-side down should be on the grill that has been preheated. The skin should be crispy and golden brown after cooking for 15 to 20 minutes. When the chicken is cooked and the internal temperature reveryes 165°F (74°C), turn it over and continue grilling for 15 to 20 minutes.

6. To keep the chicken moist and enhance the taste, occasionally basting it with the reserved marinade while cooking.

7. After it has finished cooking, take the chicken off the grill and give it some time to rest.

8. Serve the grilled chicken hot and, if you'd like, cover it with more barbecue sauce.

Nutrition Information (per serving, based on 1 leg quarter)

Calories: 400 Protein: 28g Fat: 25g
Carbohydrates: 18g Fiber: 1g

Spicy Barbecued Chicken

Preparation Time: 15 minutes

Marinating Time: 1-4 hours

Cooking Time: 30-40 minutes

Ingredients

- 4 chicken leg quarters (or a combination of chicken drumsticks and thighs)
- 1 cup of barbecue sauce (your favourite brand or homemade)
- 2 tbsp olive oil

- 2 tbsp apple cider vinegar
- 2 tbsp hot sauce (adjust as needed for desired spice level)
- 2 cloves garlic, minced
- 1 tsp smoked paprika
- 1 tsp chilli powder
- 1/2 tsp cayenne pepper (adjust as needed)
- Salt and black pepper as needed

Instructions

1. Barbecue sauce, olive oil, apple cider vinegar, hot sauce, minced garlic, smoked paprika, chilli powder, cayenne, salt, and black pepper should all be mixed in a bowl. To prepare the marinade, whisk everything together.

2. The chicken leg parts should be put in a large zip-top bag or shallow plate. To ensure the chicken is well covered, pour the marinade over it. Refrigerate for 1-4 hours to let the tastes meld, then seal the bag or cover the dish. If you need more time, marinate for at least 30 minutes.

3. Heat your grill to a moderately hot setting.

4. Take the chicken out of the marinade and save the extra for basting.

5. The skin-side down should be on the grill that has been preheated. The skin should be crispy and golden brown after cooking for 15 to 20 minutes. When the chicken is cooked and the internal temperature reveryes 165°F (74°C), turn it over and continue grilling for 15 to 20 minutes.

6. To keep the chicken moist and enhance the taste, occasionally

basting it with the reserved marinade while cooking.

7. After it has finished cooking, take the chicken off the grill and give it some time to rest.

8. Serve the hot, spicy barbecued chicken with more barbecue sauce on top.

Nutrition Information (per serving, based on 1 leg quarter)

Calories: 420 Protein: 28g Fat: 25g Carbohydrates: 19g Fiber: 1g

Glazed Meatloaf

Preparation Time: 15 minutes

Cooking Time: 1 hour 15 minutes

Total Time: 1 hour 30 minutes

Ingredients

- 1 ½ lb. ground beef
- ½ lb. ground pork
- 1 cup of breadcrumbs
- 1 onion, finely chopped
- 2 cloves garlic, minced
- 2 eggs, beaten
- ½ cup of milk
- 2 tbsp Worcestershire sauce
- 1 tbsp Dijon mustard
- 1 tsp dried thyme
- 1 tsp dried oregano
- 1 tsp salt
- ½ tsp black pepper

Glaze:

- ½ cup of ketchup
- 2 tbsp brown sugar
- 1 tbsp apple cider vinegar

Instructions

1. Preheat the oven to 350 °F.

2. Ground beef, ground pork, breadcrumbs, finely chopped onion, minced garlic, milk, Worcestershire sauce, Dijon mustard; dried thyme, dried oregano, salt, and black pepper should all be mixed in a big bowl. All of the ingredients should be well mixed.

3. Shape the meat mixture into a loaf and transfer it to a loaf pan that has been oiled.

4. Mix the ketchup, brown sugar, and apple cider vinegar in a small bowl to prepare the glaze.

5. The meatloaf's top should be covered with half of the glaze.

6. For 45 minutes, bake the meatloaf in a preheated oven.

7. Remove the meatloaf from the oven and thoroughly drain any extra fat after 45 minutes.

8. The meatloaf should be cooked until the internal temperature revereyes 160°F (71°C), which takes another 25 to 30 minutes in the oven. Spread the leftover glaze over the top of the meatloaf.

9. After cooking, remove the meatloaf from the oven and let it rest before slicing.

10. Serve the glazed meatloaf hot with your favorite side dishes, such as mashed potatoes or roasted veggies.

Nutrition Information (per serving, based on 1/8th of the meatloaf)

Calories: 320 Protein: 20g Fat: 18g Carbohydrates: 18g Fiber: 1g

Chicken with Tarragon and Lentils, Pan-Roasted

Preparation Time: 15 minutes

Cooking Time: 30 minutes

Total Time: 45 minutes

Ingredients

- 4 boneless, skinless chicken breasts
- Salt and black pepper as needed
- 2 tbsp olive oil
- 1 onion, diced
- 2 cloves garlic, minced
- 1 cup of dried green lentils
- 2 cups of low-sodium chicken broth
- 1 tsp dried tarragon
- 1/2 tsp dried thyme
- 1/2 tsp paprika
- 1/4 tsp red pepper flakes
- Fresh tarragon leaves (for garnish)

Instructions

1. Season chicken breasts with salt and pepper.
2. Over medium heat, warm up the olive oil in a skillet. Cooked the chicken breasts in the skillet for 6 to 8 minutes on every side or until they are well-cooked. The chicken should be taken out of the pan and put aside.
3. Add minced garlic and chopped onion to the same skillet. Sauté for two to three minutes or until aromatic and softening.
4. Add the lentils, chicken stock, paprika, red pepper flakes (if using), dried tarragon, and dried thyme to the pan. To blend, thoroughly stir.
5. The lentils should simmer for approximately 20 minutes, or until they are soft and have absorbed most of the liquid, with the pan covered on low heat. To avoid sticking, stir every so while.
6. Return the chicken breasts to the pan with the lentils after cooking. Cover the skillet once more for an extra five minutes of cooking to let the flavors mingle.
7. Take the skillet from the stove. Before serving, let the dish rest for a short while.
8. Add some fresh tarragon leaves as a garnish to the chicken and lentils.
9. Warmly serve the chicken with the lentils and tarragon as a main course.

Nutrition Information (per serving, based on 1 chicken breast with lentils)

Calories: 380 Protein: 45g Fat: 10g
Carbohydrates: 30g Fiber: 12g

Chicken with Lemon Pepper and Garlic

Preparation Time: 10 minutes

Cooking Time: 25-30 minutes

Total Time: 35-40 minutes

Ingredients

- 4 boneless, skinless chicken breasts
- 2 tbsp olive oil
- 2 cloves garlic, minced
- 1 tbsp lemon zest
- 1 tbsp lemon juice
- 1 tsp lemon pepper seasoning

- 1/2 tsp salt
- 1/4 tsp black pepper
- Fresh parsley, chopped (for garnish)
- Lemon wedges (for serving)

Instructions

1. Preheat the oven to 400 °F.
2. Mix the minced garlic, lemon juice, lemon zest, lemon pepper seasoning, salt, and black pepper in a small bowl.
3. Place chicken breasts in a baking dish or parchment-lined baking sheet.
4. Sprinkle the lemon pepper and garlic mixture equally over the chicken breasts after applying the olive oil. Make sure the spice is well distributed throughout the chicken using your hands or a brush.
5. The chicken should be cooked thoroughly and have an internal temperature of 165°F when placed in the oven for 25 to 30 minutes.
6. After the chicken has finished cooking, take it out of the oven and give it some time to rest.
7. Serve the chicken with lemon wedges on the side and top with freshly chopped parsley.
8. A side salad, roasted vegetables, or your favorite side dishes can be served with chicken.

Nutrition Information (per serving, based on 1 chicken breast)

Calories: 250 Protein: 30g Fat: 12g
Carbohydrates: 2g Fiber: 0g

Sweet and Sour Chicken with Rice

Preparation Time: 20 minutes

Cooking Time: 25 minutes

Total Time: 45 minutes

Ingredients

For the Sweet and Sour Sauce:

- 1/4 cup of ketchup
- 3 tbsp rice vinegar
- 3 tbsp low-sodium soy sauce
- 3 tbsp honey
- 1 tbsp cornstarch
- 1/2 cup of pineapple juice (from canned pineapple)
- 1/4 cup of water

For the Chicken:

- 1 lb. boneless, skinless chicken breast, cut into bite-sized pieces
- 1/2 cup of all-purpose flour
- 1/2 tsp salt
- 1/4 tsp black pepper
- 2 tbsp vegetable oil

For the Stir-Fry:

- 1 red bell pepper, cut into chunks
- 1 green bell pepper, cut into chunks
- 1 small onion, cut into chunks
- 1 cup of pineapple chunks
- Cooked rice (white or brown) for serving

Instructions

1. To make the sweet and sour sauce, mix the honey, cornstarch, ketchup, rice vinegar, soy sauce, pineapple

juice, and water in a small dish. Place aside.

2. Mix the flour, salt, and black pepper in a separate basin. Chicken pieces should be coated after being tossed in the flour mixture.

3. Warm the vegetable oil over medium heat in a large skillet or wok. Cook the breaded chicken pieces for 4–5 minutes on every side or until golden and well done. From the skillet, remove the cooked chicken, and put it aside.

4. Add the bell peppers and onion to the same skillet. Once they start to soften, stir-fry for 2 to 3 minutes.

5. The skillet must fry the pineapple pieces for 1-2 minutes.

6. Over the veggies in the skillet, pour the sweet and sour sauce. Cook the sauce until it thickens and coats the veggies, stirring regularly. It should take two to three minutes.

7. When you add the cooked chicken to the skillet, ensure the sweet and sour sauce is evenly distributed.

8. Take the skillet from the stove. Overcooked rice, served the sweet and sour chicken.

Nutrition Information (per serving, without rice)

Calories: 350 Protein: 25g Fat: 9g
Carbohydrates: 40g Fiber: 2g

Pasta with Vegetables

Preparation Time: 15 minutes

Cooking Time: 15 minutes

Total Time: 30 minutes

Ingredients

- 8 oz. pasta of your choice (such as penne, spaghetti, or fusilli)
- 2 tbsp olive oil
- 2 cloves garlic, minced
- 1 small onion, thinly sliced
- 1 red bell pepper, thinly sliced
- 1 yellow bell pepper, thinly sliced
- 1 zucchini, thinly sliced
- 1 cup of cherry tomatoes, halved
- 1 tsp dried basil
- 1 tsp dried oregano
- Salt and black pepper as needed
- Grated Parmesan cheese (optional for serving)
- Fresh basil leaves (for garnish)

Instructions

1. Pasta should be cooked as directed on the package until it is al dente. Drain, then set apart.

2. Olive oil should be heated in a large pan over medium heat. Sauté the onion slices for two to three minutes, or until the onion softens and the garlic is aromatic.

3. Add the sliced red and yellow bell peppers, zucchini, cherry tomatoes, dried oregano, dried basil, salt, and pepper to the skillet. To blend, thoroughly stir.

4. Stirring regularly, cook the veggies for an additional 5-7 minutes or until they are crisp-tender.

5. In the pan with the veggies, add the cooked pasta. Stir everything

together, then cook it through for one to two minutes.

6. Remove the pan from the heat and top with freshly chopped basil leaves and grated Parmesan cheese, if preferred.

7. Hot pasta with veggies can be served as a main course or a side dish with your preferred protein.

Nutrition Information

Calories: 350 Protein: 10g Fat: 10g Carbohydrates: 55g Fiber: 6g

Pumpkin Pasta Sauce

Preparation Time: 10 minutes

Cooking Time: 20 minutes

Total Time: 30 minutes

Ingredients

- 1 tbsp olive oil
- 1 small onion, finely chopped
- 2 cloves garlic, minced
- 1 cup of pumpkin puree
- 1 cup of vegetable or chicken broth
- 1/2 cup of heavy cream
- 1/4 tsp ground nutmeg
- 1/4 tsp dried sage
- Salt and black pepper as needed
- Cooked pasta of your choice (such as fettuccine or penne)
- Grated Parmesan cheese (optional for serving)
- Fresh parsley or sage leaves (for garnish)

Instructions

1. Olive oil should be heated in a large pan over medium heat. When aromatic and the onion turns translucent, add the minced garlic and the chopped onion and sauté for two to three minutes.

2. Add the pumpkin puree, chicken or vegetable broth, heavy cream, crushed nutmeg, dried sage, salt, and black pepper to the pan. To blend, thoroughly stir.

3. Stirring periodically, bring the sauce to a simmer, then lower the heat and let it cook for around 10 minutes. This enables the sauce to gradually thicken and the flavors to mix.

4. Cooked the pasta to al dente per the directions on the package while the sauce simmers. Drain, then set apart.

5. Remove the pan from the heat after the sauce has thickened. If necessary, taste and adjust the seasoning.

6. Toss the spaghetti to distribute the sauce uniformly after adding the cooked pasta to the pumpkin sauce.

7. If preferred, s

8. erve the heated pumpkin spaghetti with fresh parsley or sage leaves and grated Parmesan cheese.

Nutrition Information

Calories: 300 Protein: 5g Fat: 15g Carbohydrates: 38g Fiber: 5g

Vegan Buddha Bowl

Preparation Time: 15 minutes

Cooking Time: 25 minutes

Total Time: 40 minutes

Ingredients

For the Roasted Chickpeas:

- 15 oz.) chickpeas, drained and rinsed
- 1 tbsp olive oil
- 1 tsp smoked paprika
- 1/2 tsp garlic powder
- Salt and black pepper as needed

For the Quinoa:

- 1 cup of quinoa
- 2 cups of vegetable broth or water
- Salt as need

For the Bowl:

- 4 cups of mixed salad greens
- 1 cup of cherry tomatoes, halved
- 1 cucumber, diced
- 1 avocado, sliced
- 1/2 cup of shredded carrots
- 1/4 cup of sliced red onion
- Fresh herbs for garnish

For the Lemon-Tahini Dressing:

- 1/4 cup of tahini
- 2 tbsp fresh lemon juice
- 2 tbsp water
- 1 clove garlic, minced
- Salt and black pepper as needed

Instructions

1. Turn on the oven to 400 °F.

2. Chickpeas should be well coated with olive oil, salt, smoked paprika, garlic powder, and black pepper after being drained and washed. On a baking sheet, spread the chickpeas and bake for 25 minute or until crisp and golden brown. Place aside.
3. After thoroughly rinsing the quinoa with cold water, put it in a saucepan with water or vegetable broth. Bring to a boil, lower the heat to a simmer, cover the pan, and cook the quinoa for 15 to 20 minutes, depending on how quickly the liquid is absorbed. With a fork, fluff and set aside.
4. Blend the tahini, water, fresh lemon juice, minced garlic, salt, and black pepper in a bowl. Place aside.
5. Divide the mixed salad greens among the four bowls to construct the bowl. Add cooked quinoa, roasted chickpeas, cucumber, cherry tomatoes, sliced avocados, shredded carrots, and thinly sliced red onions as garnishes.
6. Sprinkle the bowl with fresh herbs, then drizzle the lemon-tahini dressing.
7. The vegan Buddha dish should be served right away.

Nutrition Information (per serving)

Calories: 400 Protein: 15g Fat: 20g
Carbohydrates: 45g Fiber: 12g

Halibut with Tomato Salsa

Preparation Time: 15 minutes

Cooking Time: 12-15 minutes

Total Time: 27-30 minutes

Ingredients

- 4 halibut fillets (about 6 oz. every)
- 2 tbsp olive oil
- Salt and black pepper as needed
- For the Tomato Salsa:
- 1 cup of diced tomatoes
- 1/4 cup of diced red onion
- 1/4 cup of chopped fresh cilantro
- 1 tbsp fresh lime juice
- 1 jalapeño pepper, seeds removed and finely chopped (optional for added heat)
- Salt as need

Instructions

1. Preheat the oven to 400 °F.
2. On both sides, season the halibut fillets with salt and black pepper.
3. Heat the olive oil over medium heat in an oven-safe skillet. The halibut fillets should be cooked in the skillet for 3 to 4 minutes on every side or until barely browned.
4. When the halibut is cooked and flakes readily with a fork, put the pan in the preheated oven for 6 to 8 minutes.
5. Make the tomato salsa while the halibut is baking. Mix the diced tomatoes, red onion, cilantro, lime juice, salt, and jalapenos (if using) in a bowl. To blend, thoroughly stir.
6. Remove the pan from the oven after the halibut has finished cooking.
7. Hot halibut should be served with tomato salsa on top.

Nutrition Information (per serving, based on 1 halibut fillet with salsa)

Calories: 250 Protein: 30g Fat: 12g Carbohydrates: 5g Fiber: 1g

Herb-Crust Cod

Preparation Time: 10 minutes

Cooking Time: 12-15 minutes

Total Time: 22-25 minutes

Ingredients

- 4 cod fillets (about 6 oz. every)
- 2 tbsp olive oil
- 1 cup of breadcrumbs (can use panko or homemade)
- 2 tbsp fresh parsley, chopped
- 1 tbsp fresh dill, chopped
- 1 tbsp fresh thyme leaves
- 1 tbsp lemon zest
- 1 tsp garlic powder
- Salt and black pepper as needed
- Lemon wedges (for serving)

Instructions

1. Turn on the oven to 425 °F.
2. To remove any extra moisture, pat the cod fillets dry with a paper towel.
3. Breadcrumbs, chopped parsley, dill, chopped thyme leaves, lemon zest, garlic powder, salt, and black pepper should all be mixed in a small basin. The herbs and seasonings should be well mixed with the breadcrumbs.

4. Cover both sides of every cod fillet with olive oil as you brush it on.
5. Before being coated, every fillet should be gently dipped into the herb breadcrumb mixture.
6. Cod fillets with a herb crust should be put on a baking sheet covered with parchment paper or a baking dish that has been lightly oiled.
7. For 12 to 15 minutes, or until the cod is opaque and flakes readily with a fork, bake the cod in the preheated oven.
8. After cooking, take the cod out of the oven and give it time to rest.
9. Hot herb-crusted cod should be served with lemon wedges nearby for squeezing over the fish.

Nutrition Information (per serving, based on 1 cod fillet)

Calories: 300 Protein: 25g Fat: 10g
Carbohydrates: 25g Fiber: 2g

Honey-Crusted Chicken

Preparation Time: 15 minutes

Cooking Time: 25-30 minutes

Total Time: 40-45 minutes

Ingredients

- 4 boneless, skinless chicken breasts
- 1/4 cup of honey
- 2 tbsp Dijon mustard
- 1 tbsp olive oil
- 1 cup of breadcrumbs (regular or panko)
- 1 tsp dried thyme
- 1/2 tsp garlic powder
- Salt and black pepper as needed

- Fresh parsley or thyme leaves (for garnish)

Instructions

1. Set your oven's temperature to 375°F (190°C).
2. Mix the honey, Dijon mustard, and olive oil in a small bowl.
3. Mix the breadcrumbs, dried thyme, garlic powder, salt, and black pepper in a separate bowl.
4. Spread the honey-mustard mixture on every chicken breast after dipping it in it.
5. Honey-coated chicken breasts are added to the breadcrumb mixture and gently pressed to help the breadcrumbs stick to the chicken.
6. Put the coated chicken breasts in a greased baking dish or parchment sheet.
7. When the chicken is golden brown and the internal temperature reaches 165°F (74°C), bake it in the preheated oven for 25-30 minutes.
8. After the chicken has finished cooking, take it out of the oven and give it some time to rest.
9. Hot honey-crusted chicken should be served with fresh parsley, or thyme leaves as a garnish.

Nutrition Information (per serving, based on 1 chicken breast)

Calories: 300 Protein: 25g Fat: 6g
Carbohydrates: 35g Fiber: 2g

Zucchini-Chickpea Burgers

Preparation Time: 20 minutes

Cooking Time: 15 minutes

Total Time: 35 minutes

Ingredients

- 2 cups of grated zucchini (about 2 medium zucchini)
- 15 oz. chickpeas, drained and rinsed
- 1/2 cup of breadcrumbs (regular or gluten-free)
- 1/4 cup of chopped fresh parsley
- 2 cloves garlic, minced
- 1 tsp ground cumin
- 1/2 tsp paprika
- Salt and black pepper as needed
- 2 tbsp olive oil (for cooking)
- Burger buns and desired toppings for serving

Instructions

1. Grate the zucchini and place it in a cheesecloth or clean kitchen towel. Squeeze the zucchini to remove any extra liquid. This step aids in keeping the burgers from getting overly soggy.
2. Mash the drained chickpeas in a large basin with a fork or potato masher until they're mostly smooth.
3. Grated zucchini, breadcrumbs, parsley that has been chopped, minced garlic, cumin, paprika, salt, and black pepper should all be added to the bowl. All of the ingredients should be well mixed.
4. Form the mixture into burger patties using about 1/4 to 1/3 cup of the ingredients per patty. You should be able to make 6 patties.
5. Over medium heat, warm the olive oil in a skillet. The zucchini-chickpea patties should be cooked in the skillet for 4-5 minutes on every side or until crispy and golden.
6. When the burgers have finished cooking, take them from the skillet and give them some time to rest.
7. Top the zucchini-chickpea patties on burger buns with your preferred lettuce, tomato, avocado, and sauces.

Nutrition Information

Calories: 120 Protein: 5g Fat: 4g
Carbohydrates: 17g Fiber: 4g

Chicken Tenders with Bagel Seasoning

Preparation Time: 15 minutes

Cooking Time: 15-20 minutes

Total Time: 30-35 minutes

Ingredients

- 1 lb. chicken tenders
- 1/2 cup of all-purpose flour
- 2 eggs, beaten
- 1 cup of breadcrumbs
- 2 tbsp everything bagel seasoning
- Salt and black pepper as needed
- Cooking spray or olive oil for greasing

Instructions

1. Preheat the oven to 425 °F.

2. Prepare three shallow basins or plates with flour, beaten eggs, breadcrumbs mixed with bagel seasoning, salt, and black pepper.
3. Every chicken tender should be floured, and any excess should be shaken off. After that, dip it into the beaten eggs and let any extra drop off. Lastly, sprinkle it with the breadcrumb mixture and lightly press it to help the breadcrumbs stick to the chicken.
4. Put the coated chicken tenders on a parchment paper or oiled baking sheet.
5. Cooking spray or olive oil should be lightly drizzled over the chicken tenders. In the oven, this will aid in their browning and crisping.
6. The chicken tenders should be baked for 15 to 20 minutes in a preheated oven or until well cooked. The inside should be 165°F (74°C) or higher.
7. Once done, take the chicken tenders out of the oven and give them a moment to rest.
8. With your preferred dipping sauces, serve the chicken tenders hot as a main meal or as a finger snack.

Nutrition Information

Calories: 250 Protein: 30g Fat: 8g
Carbohydrates: 15g Fiber: 1g

Honey-Garlic Chicken Thighs

Preparation Time: 10 minutes

Marinating Time: 1-4 hours (optional)

Cooking Time: 25-30 minutes

Total Time: 35 minutes to 4 hours 40 minutes

Ingredients

- 8 bone-in, skin-on chicken thighs
- 1/4 cup of soy sauce
- 1/4 cup of honey
- 3 tbsp rice vinegar
- 3 cloves garlic, minced
- 1 tsp grated ginger
- 1/2 tsp red pepper flakes
- Salt and black pepper as needed
- Chopped green onions or sesame seeds for garnish

Instructions

1. Soy sauce, honey, rice vinegar, grated ginger, chopped garlic, red pepper flakes (if used), salt, and black pepper should all be mixed in a bowl.
2. Put the chicken thighs in a ziplock bag or a shallow plate. Ensure every thigh of the chicken is covered in the honey-garlic marinade before pouring it over. If you have the time, let the food marinate in the fridge for 1-4 hours. If time is of the essence, you can omit the marinating phase.
3. Turn on the oven to 425 °F.
4. Cast iron or a skillet safe for the oven should be heated to a high temperature. The chicken thighs should be removed from the

marinade and placed skin-side down on the heated skillet, keeping the marinade aside for later use. The skin of the chicken should be browned and crispy after 3–4 minutes of searing.

5. Pour the reserved marinade over the chicken thighs after turning them over. Due to the marinade, some sizzling may occur. The skillet should be placed in the preheated oven.

6. The chicken thighs should be baked for 20 to 25 minutes, or until the juices flow clear and the internal temperature of the chicken reaches 165°F (74°C).

7. After the chicken has finished cooking, take the pan out of the oven and rest for a few minutes.

8. Hot honey-garlic chicken thighs should be served with sesame seeds or chopped green onions as a garnish. They may be served with rice, steamed veggies, or other side dishes.

Nutrition Information (per serving, based on 2 chicken thighs)

Calories: 420 Protein: 28g Fat: 25g Carbohydrates: 17g Fiber: 0g

CHAPTER 4: MEAT RECIPES

Spiced Beef

Preparation Time: 15 minutes

Cooking Time: 20-25 minutes

Total Time: 35-40 minutes

Ingredients

- 1 lb. ground beef
- 1 onion, finely chopped
- 2 cloves garlic, minced
- 1 tsp ground cumin
- 1 tsp ground coriander
- 1/2 tsp paprika
- 1/4 tsp ground cinnamon
- 1/4 tsp cayenne pepper (adjust as needed)
- Salt and black pepper as needed
- 2 tbsp olive oil
- Fresh cilantro or parsley for garnish (optional)

Instructions

1. Ground beef, minced garlic, ground cumin, coriander, paprika, ground cinnamon, salt, cayenne pepper, and black pepper are all mixed in a bowl. All of the ingredients should be well mixed.

2. Your chosen size of meatballs or patties may be made using the seasoned beef mixture.

3. Over medium heat, warm the olive oil in a large skillet. Working in batches, if necessary, to prevent overflowing the skillet, add the seasoned beef patties or meatballs.

4. Cook the seasoned meat until browned and well cooked, about 5-7

minutes per side. For ground beef, make sure the internal temperature reaches 160°F (71°C).

5. After it has finished cooking, take the seasoned meat out of the skillet and give it some time to rest.

6. If preferred, garnish the hot spicy beef with fresh cilantro or parsley. It may be used as filler for wraps or sandwiches or as a main meal with rice or couscous.

Nutrition Information

Calories: 250 Protein: 20g Fat: 18g
Carbohydrates: 4g Fiber: 1g

Tomato Beef

Preparation Time: 15 minutes

Cooking Time: 1 hour 30 minutes

Total Time: 1 hour 45 minutes

Ingredients

- 1.5 lb. beef stew meat, cut into bite-sized pieces
- 1 onion, diced
- 2 cloves garlic, minced
- 2 tbsp olive oil
- 1 can (14 oz.) diced tomatoes
- 1 can (6 oz.) tomato paste
- 1 cup of beef broth
- 1 tsp dried basil
- 1 tsp dried oregano
- 1/2 tsp dried thyme
- Salt and black pepper as needed
- Fresh parsley for garnish (optional)

Instructions

1. The olive oil should be heated over medium heat in a big saucepan or Dutch oven. When aromatic and the onion turns translucent, add the chopped onion and the minced garlic and sauté for two to three minutes.

2. Brown the beef stew meat completely in the saucepan before adding it. It will take five to seven minutes. The meat should be taken out of the saucepan and kept aside.

3. Add the diced tomatoes and their juice, tomato paste, beef broth, dried thyme, dried oregano, dried basil, and salt to the same saucepan. To blend, thoroughly stir.

4. Add the browned meat back to the saucepan with the tomato mixture coated on top.

5. Heat should be turned down once the mixture comes to a boil. For one and a half hours, or until the meat is tender and the flavors are well-balanced, simmer the dish with the lid on.

6. To prevent sticking, stir occasionally while cooking.

7. Remove the saucepan from the heat after the steak is done and tender. Give the tomato meat some time to rest.

8. If preferred, top the tomato beef with fresh parsley before serving. Rice, spaghetti, or mashed potatoes go nicely with this recipe.

Nutrition Information

Calories: 350 Protein: 30g Fat: 18g
Carbohydrates: 16g Fiber: 4g

Beef Tenderloin Medallions with Yogurt Sauce

Preparation Time: 15 minutes

Cooking Time: 10-12 minutes

Total Time: 25-27 minutes

Ingredients

For the Beef Tenderloin:

- 1 lb. beef tenderloin, cut into 1-inch thick medallions
- 2 tbsp olive oil
- 1 tsp dried thyme
- 1 tsp dried rosemary
- Salt and black pepper as needed

For the Yogurt Sauce:

- 1 cup of Greek yogurt
- 2 tbsp fresh lemon juice
- 1 clove garlic, minced
- 1 tbsp chopped fresh dill
- Salt and black pepper as needed

Instructions

1. Heat your skillet or grill to a medium-high setting.
2. The dried thyme, salt, rosemary, and black pepper should all be mixed in a small dish. The medallions of beef tenderloin should be rubbed with this mixture on both sides.
3. Olive oil should be applied to the medallions and massaged into the flesh.
4. Cook the beef medallions in the skillet or on the grill. Cook for around 4-6 minutes on every side or until the food is cooked to your preference. Aim for an internal temperature of 130–135°F for medium-rare.
5. Make the yogurt sauce while the meat cooks. Greek yogurt, fresh lemon juice, minced garlic, finely chopped fresh dill, salt, and black pepper should all be mixed in a different bowl. To blend, thoroughly stir.
6. When the beef tenderloin medallions are cooked to your preference, please turn off the heat and let them a few minutes to rest.
7. Serve the yogurt sauce beside the heated beef tenderloin medallions.
8. This meal goes well with roasted veggies, a side salad, or any other dish you choose.

Nutrition Information

Calories: 300 Protein: 30g Fat: 18g
Carbohydrates: 4g Fiber: 1g

Mustardy Zucchini Beef Burger

Preparation Time: 15 minutes

Cooking Time: 12-15 minutes

Total Time: 27-30 minutes

Ingredients

For the Burgers:

- 1 lb. ground beef
- 1 cup of grated zucchini
- 1/4 cup of breadcrumbs (regular or gluten-free)
- 2 tbsp Dijon mustard
- 1 tbsp Worcestershire sauce
- 1 clove garlic, minced

- 1 tsp dried oregano
- Salt and black pepper as needed
- Burger buns and desired toppings for serving

For the Mustard Sauce:

- 1/4 cup of mayonnaise
- 2 tbsp Dijon mustard
- 1 tbsp honey

Instructions

1. Ground beef, grated zucchini, breadcrumbs, Dijon mustard, Worcestershire sauce, chopped garlic, dried oregano, salt, and black pepper should all be mixed in a large bowl. All of the ingredients should be well mixed.
2. Form the mixture into burger patties using about 1/4 to 1/3 cup of the ingredients per patty. You should be able to produce 4-6 patties.
3. Heat up your skillet or grill to medium-high.
4. The burgers should be cooked on every side for 4–5 minutes or until cooked to your preference.
5. Make the mustard sauce while the burgers are cooking. Mayonnaise, Dijon mustard, and honey should be blended in a small basin.
6. Once the burgers are done cooking, please turn off the heat and let them a few minutes to rest.
7. Top the mustard-flavored beef patties on burger buns with your preferred toppings and a dab of the mustard sauce.

Nutrition Information

Calories: 300 Protein: 25g Fat: 20g
Carbohydrates: 6g Fiber: 1g

Garlicky Beef Tenderloin with Artichoke

Preparation time: 15 minutes

Cooking time: 25 minutes

Servings: 4

Ingredients

- 1 ½ lb. beef tenderloin, trimmed and cut into 4 steaks
- 4 cloves garlic, minced
- 2 tbsp olive oil
- 1 tsp dried thyme
- Salt and pepper as needed
- 1 can artichoke hearts, drained and quartered
- 1 tbsp butter
- 2 tbsp fresh parsley, chopped

Instructions

1. Turn on the oven to 400 °F.
2. Mix the minced garlic, olive oil, dried thyme, salt, and pepper in a small bowl. The beef tenderloin steaks should be uniformly covered with this mixture on both sides.
3. Heat a skillet that can be used in the oven to medium-high. The steaks should be added to the heated skillet and seared for 2 minutes on every side or until well browned.
4. Place the steak-containing pan in the preheated oven. For medium-rare, cook for 10 to 12 minutes, or modify the cooking time to your preferred degree of doneness.
5. Melt the butter in a separate pan over medium heat as the steaks cook. Add the artichoke hearts and cook them for 5 minutes or so or until they are soft.

6. The beef tenderloin should be removed from the oven and placed on a chopping board. Give it a few minutes to relax.
7. Beef tenderloin steaks should be thinly sliced.
8. Place the sliced beef on serving platters, followed by the artichoke hearts that have been browned. Add fresh parsley as a garnish.

Nutrition Information (per serving)

Calories: 380 Protein: 36g Fat: 23g
Carbohydrates: 6g Fiber: 3g Sugar: 1g
Sodium: 470mg

Beef with Spicy Vegetable Stir-Fry

Preparation time: 15 minutes

Cooking time: 15 minutes

Servings: 4

Ingredients

- 1 lb. beef sirloin, thinly sliced
- 2 tbsp soy sauce
- 2 tbsp oyster sauce
- 1 tbsp hoisin sauce
- 1 tbsp sriracha sauce (adjust as needed)
- 2 tbsp vegetable oil, divided
- 3 cloves garlic, minced
- 1 tsp fresh ginger, grated
- 1 medium onion, thinly sliced
- 1 red bell pepper, thinly sliced
- 1 yellow bell pepper, thinly sliced
- 1 small broccoli head, cut into florets
- 1 medium carrot, thinly sliced
- 1 cup of snap peas

- 2 green onions, chopped
- Sesame seeds for garnish (optional)

Instructions

1. The soy sauce, oyster sauce, hoisin sauce, and sriracha sauce should all be mixed in a bowl. Sliced meat should then be added and well-coated. 10 minutes should be set up for marinating.
2. Heat 1 tbsp of vegetable oil over high heat in a large skillet or wok. Stir-fry the beef with the marinade for 3 to 4 minutes or until it is browned. Please remove the meat from the skillet and set it aside.
3. Add the final tbsp of vegetable oil to the same skillet. The grated ginger and chopped garlic should heat for approximately a minute to become aromatic.
4. Add sliced onions, red and yellow bell peppers, broccoli florets, carrots, and snap peas to the pan. Vegetables should be stir-fried for 4-5 minutes or until crisp-tender.
5. Toss the cooked meat and veggies back into the skillet. To fully heat everything, cook for a further two to three minutes.
6. Give the stir-fry one last toss after adding the chopped green onions.
7. Over hot steaming rice or noodles, serve the beef stir-fry. If desired, add sesame seeds as a garnish.

Nutrition Information (per serving)

Calories: 320 Protein: 26g Fat: 15g
Carbohydrates: 20g Fiber: 6g Sugar: 9g

Beef Tenderloin with Balsamic Tomatoes

Preparation time: 15 minutes

Cooking time: 25 minutes

Servings: 4

Ingredients

- 1 ½ lb. beef tenderloin, trimmed and tied
- Salt and pepper as needed
- 2 tbsp olive oil
- 2 tbsp balsamic vinegar
- 2 cloves garlic, minced
- 1 pint cherry tomatoes, halved
- 1 tbsp fresh basil, chopped
- 1 tbsp fresh parsley, chopped

Instructions

1. Turn on the oven to 425 °F.
2. On all sides, season the beef tenderloin with salt and pepper.
3. Heat a skillet that can be used in the oven to medium-high. The beef tenderloin should be seared until browned, adding olive oil as needed. Overall, this should take roughly 4-5 minutes.
4. Transfer the beef tenderloin-containing pan to the preheated oven. For medium-rare, roast for about 15 minutes, or modify the cooking time to your preferred degree of doneness.
5. Prepare the balsamic tomatoes while the meat is roasting. Balsamic vinegar should be heated over medium heat in a separate skillet. Once aromatic, add the minced garlic and simmer for 1 minute.
6. While stirring occasionally, add the cherry tomatoes to the skillet and simmer for 5-7 minutes or until they soften and release juices.
7. The beef tenderloin in the pan should be removed from the oven and placed on a chopping board. Give it a few minutes to relax.
8. The beef tenderloin should be cut into thick pieces.
9. Arrange the beef tenderloin slices and top with the balsamic tomatoes on a platter. Add fresh parsley and basil as a garnish.

Nutrition Information (per serving)

Calories: 350 Protein: 34g Fat: 20g
Carbohydrates: 6g Fiber: 1g Sugar: 4g
Sodium: 180mg

Fajita-Style Beef Tacos

Preparation time: 15 minutes

Marinating time: 30 minutes

Cooking time: 15 minutes

Servings: 4

Ingredients

For the marinade:

- 1 lb. beef flank steak, thinly sliced
- 2 tbsp lime juice
- 2 tbsp olive oil
- 2 cloves garlic, minced
- 1 tsp ground cumin
- 1 tsp chilli powder
- 1/2 tsp smoked paprika
- 1/2 tsp salt
- 1/4 tsp black pepper

For the tacos:

- 8 small flour tortillas

- 1 medium onion, thinly sliced
- 1 red bell pepper, thinly sliced
- 1 green bell pepper, thinly sliced
- 2 tbsp vegetable oil
- Salt and pepper as needed
- Optional toppings: chopped fresh cilantro, sour cream, guacamole, salsa

Instructions

1. Mix the lime juice, olive oil, cumin, chilli powder, smoked paprika, salt, and black pepper in a bowl. Sliced flank steak made of beef should be added and coated well. Refrigerate the meat for at least 30 minutes to let it marinate.
2. Over medium-high heat, preheat a large pan or skillet. The flour tortillas should be warmed through on both sides until they are flexible. They may stay warm by being wrapped in a fresh kitchen towel.
3. Heat the vegetable oil to a medium-high temperature in the same skillet or griddle. Bell peppers and onion, in slices, are added. The veggies should be slightly softened and gently browned after cooking for 5-7 minutes with fitful tossing. Add pepper and salt as needed when seasoning.
4. The veggies should be taken out of the skillet and put aside. Add the marinated beef flank steak to the same skillet and cook for 3–4 minutes on every side, depending on how done you want your steak.
5. After taking the steak out of the skillet, give it some time to rest. Cut it into long, thin pieces.
6. Place beef slices on every heated tortilla before assembling the tacos. Add the grilled bell peppers and

onion on top. Add any preferred toppings, such as sour cream, guacamole, chopped cilantro, or salsa.
7. Serve the fajita-style beef tacos immediately, and enjoy!

Nutrition Information (per serving, without toppings)

Calories: 420 Protein: 28g Fat: 17g
Carbohydrates: 40g Fiber: 3g

One-Pot Spinach Beef Soup

Preparation time: 15 minutes

Cooking time: 30 minutes

Servings: 4

Ingredients

- 1 lb. beef stew meat, cut into bite-sized pieces
- 1 tbsp olive oil
- 1 medium onion, diced
- 2 cloves garlic, minced
- 2 carrots, peeled and sliced
- 2 celery stalks, sliced
- 4 cups of beef broth
- 1 cup of water
- 1 tsp dried thyme
- 1 tsp dried oregano
- 1 bay leaf
- 4 cups of fresh spinach leaves
- Salt and pepper as needed

Instructions

1. Heat the olive oil over medium heat in a big saucepan or Dutch oven. Brown the beef stew meat with the

addition on both sides. Take the beef out of the saucepan, then set it aside.

2. The diced onion, minced garlic, sliced carrots, and sliced celery should all be placed in the same saucepan. The veggies should start to soften after 5 minutes of sautéing.

3. Put the meat back in the saucepan and add the water and beef broth. Add the bay leaf, dried thyme, and dried oregano. Add pepper and salt as needed when seasoning.

4. Once the soup has reached a rolling boil, turn down the heat. The soup should boil for 20 minutes with the lid on so the flavors can mingle and the meat can grow soft.

5. Bay leaf should be taken out of the soup. Fresh spinach leaves are added and cooked for two to three minutes or until the spinach wilts.

6. If necessary, check the soup's flavor and season as needed.

7. Serve hot, and spoon the spinach beef soup into dishes.

Nutrition Information (per serving)

Calories: 280 Protein: 28g Fat: 12g
Carbohydrates: 14g Fiber: 4g Sugar: 5g
Sodium: 970mg

Sesame Beef Skewers

Preparation time: 15 minutes

Marinating time: 30 minutes

Cooking time: 10 minutes. Servings: 4

Ingredients

- 1 lb. beef sirloin, cut into thin strips
- 3 tbsp soy sauce
- 2 tbsp sesame oil
- 2 tbsp honey
- 2 cloves garlic, minced
- 1 tbsp grated fresh ginger
- 2 tbsp toasted sesame seeds
- 1 tbsp vegetable oil (for grilling)
- Optional garnish: chopped green onions

Instructions

1. Soy sauce, sesame oil, honey, grated ginger, chopped garlic, and toasted sesame seeds should all be mixed in a bowl. When the meat strips are well coated, add them to the bowl and mix again. Refrigerate the meat for at least 30 minutes before serving.

2. Set the temperature of your grill or grill pan to medium-high.

3. I am making sure to allow some room between every piece and thread the marinated beef strips onto the skewers.

4. To avoid sticking, lightly grease the grill grates or pan with vegetable oil. The beef skewers should be cooked on the grill for 3–4 minutes on every side or until cooked to your preference.

5. The beef skewers should be taken from the grill and given time to rest.

6. If desired, top the hot sesame beef skewers with chopped green onions.

Nutrition Information (per serving, without garnish)

Calories: 280 Protein: 25g Fat: 15g
Carbohydrates: 10g Fiber: 1g Sugar: 8g
Sodium: 760mg

Best Lasagna Soup

Preparation time: 15 minutes

Cooking time: 40 minutes

Servings: 6

Ingredients

- 1 lb. ground beef
- 1 onion, diced
- 3 cloves garlic, minced
- 1 can (14.5 oz) diced tomatoes
- 1 can (8 oz) tomato sauce
- 4 cups of beef broth
- 1 cup of water
- 1 tsp dried basil
- 1 tsp dried oregano
- 1/2 tsp salt
- 1/4 tsp black pepper
- 8 lasagna noodles broken into small pieces
- 1 cup of ricotta cheese
- 1/2 cup of shredded mozzarella cheese
- Fresh basil leaves, for garnish (optional)

Instructions

1. Cook the ground beef until browned over medium-high heat in a big saucepan or Dutch oven. Remove any extra oil.
2. Add the minced garlic and onion to the saucepan with the cooked meat. The onion should turn transparent after 2 to 3 minutes of cooking.
3. Add salt, black pepper, dried oregano, dry basil, water, tomato sauce, chopped tomatoes, and water. The soup should be heated to a rolling boil before being simmered for 20 minutes on low heat.
4. Cook the lasagna noodles in the meantime per the directions on the box. Drain the cooked food, and then set it aside.
5. To enable the cooked lasagna noodle pieces to soften and absorb the flavors, add them to the soup and boil it for an additional 10 minutes.
6. Ricotta cheese should be mixed with a little salt and black pepper in a small bowl.
7. Pour the soup into dishes to serve. Add a dollop of the ricotta cheese mixture and some shredded mozzarella cheese on the top of every dish. If desired, garnish with fresh basil leaves.

Nutrition Information (per serving)

Calories: 380 Protein: 25g Fat: 15g
Carbohydrates: 35g Fiber: 3g Sugar: 6g
Sodium: 900mg

CHAPTER 5: FISH AND SEAFOOD RECIPES

Catfish with Egg Pecans

Preparation time: 15 minutes

Cooking time: 20 minutes

Servings: 4

Ingredients

- 4 catfish fillets
- 1/2 cup of all-purpose flour
- 2 eggs, beaten
- 1 cup of pecans, finely chopped
- 1/4 cup of breadcrumbs
- 1/2 tsp salt
- 1/4 tsp black pepper
- 1/4 tsp paprika
- 2 tbsp vegetable oil
- Lemon wedges for serving

Instructions

1. Preheat your oven to 375°F.
2. Use paper towels to pat the catfish fillets dry gently. Add salt and black pepper as needed.
3. A shallow dish should contain all-purpose flour. Take every catfish fillet and uniformly cover both sides with flour. Clear away any extra flour.
4. Mix the finely chopped nuts, breadcrumbs, salt, black pepper, and paprika in a separate shallow dish.
5. Every floured catfish fillet should be dipped into the beaten eggs before being covered in the pecan breadcrumb mixture and gently pressed to adhere.
6. In an oven-safe skillet set over medium heat, warm the vegetable oil. The breaded catfish fillets should be cooked in the skillet for 3–4 minutes on every side or until golden.
7. The catfish fillets should be cooked through and flaky after an additional 10 to 12 minutes of baking in the preheated oven.
8. After removing the pan from the oven, give the catfish time to rest.
9. Catfish fillets should be served hot, along with lemon wedges for squeezing over the top.

Nutrition Information (per serving)

Calories: 420 Protein: 24g Fat: 30g
Carbohydrates: 14g Fiber: 4g Sugar: 1g
Sodium: 380mg

Roast Salmon with Tarragon

Preparation time: 10 minutes

Cooking time: 15 minutes

Servings: 4

Ingredients

- 4 salmon fillets (6 oz. every)
- 2 tbsp olive oil
- 2 tbsp fresh tarragon leaves, chopped
- 2 cloves garlic, minced
- 1 lemon, zested and juiced
- Salt and pepper as needed

Instructions

1. Preheat your oven to 425°F.
2. Put the salmon fillets on a baking sheet with aluminium foil or parchment paper.
3. Olive oil, minced garlic, lemon juice, lemon zest, chopped tarragon leaves, salt, and pepper should all be mixed in a small bowl. To make a marinade, stir thoroughly.
4. Salmon fillets should be evenly coated on both sides with the marinade mixture by brushing it on.
5. When the salmon is cooked through and flakes easily with a fork, roast it in the preheated oven for 12 to 15 minutes.
6. The salmon should be taken out of the oven and rested.
7. Add more fresh tarragon leaves and lemon wedges to the hot roast salmon before serving.

Nutrition Information (per serving)

Calories: 350 Protein: 34g Fat: 22g
Carbohydrates: 2g Fiber: 1g Sugar: 0g
Sodium: 150mg

Pasta with Lemon Spiced Shrimp and Cheese

Preparation time: 15 minutes

Cooking time: 15 minutes

Servings: 4

Ingredients

- 8 oz. pasta (linguine or spaghetti)
- 1 lb. shrimp, peeled and deveined
- 2 tbsp olive oil
- 4 cloves garlic, minced
- 1 tsp red pepper flakes (adjust as needed)
- Zest and juice of 1 lemon
- 1/2 cup of grated Parmesan cheese
- 1/4 cup of chopped fresh parsley
- Salt and pepper as needed

Instructions

1. As directed on the packaging, cook the pasta until it is al dente. Drain and reserve.
2. Melt the olive oil in a large pan over medium-high heat. Red pepper flakes and chopped garlic should heat for approximately a minute to become aromatic.
3. The shrimp should be pink and cooked through after being added to the skillet and cooked for two to three minutes on every side. The cooked shrimp should be taken out of the skillet and put aside.
4. Add the cooked pasta to the skillet and stir in the garlic-infused oil. Add the lemon juice, zest, Parmesan cheese, and chopped parsley after adding the lemon juice. To mix and coat the pasta, toss thoroughly.
5. Re-add the cooked shrimp to the pan and toss the pasta with them.
6. Add pepper and salt as needed when seasoning.
7. Top the cooked pasta with cheese and shrimp seasoned with lemon if preferred. Additional Parmesan cheese may also be added.

Nutrition Information (per serving)

Calories: 450 Protein: 35g Fat: 14g
Carbohydrates: 46g Fiber: 3g Sugar: 2g
Sodium: 440mg

Tomatoes with Tilapia Tacos

Preparation time: 20 minutes

Cooking time: 15 minutes

Servings: 4

Ingredients

- 1 lb. tilapia fillets
- 2 tbsp olive oil
- 1 tsp chilli powder
- 1/2 tsp ground cumin
- 1/2 tsp paprika
- 1/4 tsp garlic powder
- Salt and pepper as needed
- 8 small flour tortillas
- 1 cup of cherry tomatoes, halved
- 1/4 cup of red onion, finely chopped
- 1/4 cup of fresh cilantro, chopped
- Juice of 1 lime
- Optional toppings: sliced avocado, sour cream, hot sauce

Instructions

1. Preheat your oven to 400°F.
2. Put the tilapia fillets on a baking sheet with aluminium foil or parchment paper.
3. Mix the chilli powder, cumin, paprika, garlic powder, olive oil, salt, and pepper in a small bowl. Make a spice mixture by stirring thoroughly.
4. The tilapia fillets should be well coated with the spice mixture after being brushed over both sides.
5. The fish should bake in the oven for 12 to 15 minutes or until a fork can easily pierce it.
6. Tilapia should be taken out of the oven and given time to cool. Use a fork to tear the fried tilapia into little pieces.
7. Cherry tomatoes cut in half, red onion, cilantro, and lime juice should all be mixed in a bowl. Mix well by tossing.
8. The flour tortillas should be warmed in a microwave or a dry pan until they are flexible and soft.
9. Fill every tortilla with fish flakes and top with the tomato mixture to assemble the tacos. Add any preferred toppings, such as sour cream, spicy sauce, or slices of avocado.

Nutrition Information (per serving, without toppings)

Calories: 320 Protein: 30g Fat: 12g
Carbohydrates: 26g Fiber: 4g Sugar: 3g
Sodium: 260mg

Garlic-Baked Flounder

Preparation time: 10 minutes

Cooking time: 15 minutes

Servings: 4

Ingredients

- 4 flounder fillets (about 6 oz. every)
- 4 cloves garlic, minced
- 2 tbsp fresh lemon juice
- 2 tbsp olive oil
- 1/4 tsp salt
- 1/4 tsp black pepper
- 1/4 tsp paprika
- 2 tbsp fresh parsley, chopped
- Lemon wedges for serving

Instructions

1. Preheat your oven to 400°F (200°C).
2. Put the flounder fillets on a baking sheet with aluminum foil or parchment paper.
3. The minced garlic, lemon juice, olive oil, salt, black pepper, and paprika should all be mixed in a small bowl. To make a marinade for garlic, stir thoroughly.
4. The flounder fillets should be nicely coated on both sides with the garlic marinade.
5. When tested with a fork, the flounder should bake in the preheated oven for 12 to 15 minutes or until opaque and flaky.
6. After removing the flounder from the oven, top with the chopped fresh parsley.
7. Serve the hot garlic-baked flounder with lemon wedges on the side to squeeze over the top.

Nutrition Information (per serving)

Calories: 190 Protein: 28g Fat: 8g
Carbohydrates: 1g Fiber: 0g Sugar: 0g
Sodium: 190mg

Seafood Dip

Preparation time: 15 minutes

Cooking time: 15 minutes

Servings: 8

Ingredients

- 8 oz. cream cheese, softened
- 1/2 cup of mayonnaise
- 1/2 cup of sour cream
- 1/2 cup of grated Parmesan cheese
- 1/2 cup of shredded mozzarella cheese
- 1/2 cup of cooked shrimp, chopped
- 1/2 cup of lump crab meat
- 1/4 cup of chopped green onions
- 2 cloves garlic, minced
- 1 tbsp lemon juice
- 1/2 tsp Worcestershire sauce
- 1/2 tsp Old Bay seasoning
- Salt and pepper as needed

Instructions

1. Preheat your oven to 375°F (190°C).
2. Melted cream cheese, mayonnaise, sour cream, grated Parmesan cheese, shredded mozzarella cheese, chopped shrimp, lump crab meat, green onions, minced garlic, lemon juice, Worcestershire sauce, Old Bay seasoning, salt, and pepper should all be mixed in a mixing dish. Mix items thoroughly together until mixed.
3. Spread the ingredients equally in a pan that can go in the oven or a baking dish.
4. For 15 minutes, or until it is hot and bubbling, bake the seafood dip in the preheated oven.
5. The dip should be removed from the oven and cooled before serving.
6. Serve the seafood dip warm with the dippers of your choice, such as crackers, toasted baguette slices, or veggie sticks.

Nutrition Information (per serving)

Calories: 210 Protein: 8g Fat: 19g
Carbohydrates: 2g Fiber: 0g Sugar: 1g
Sodium: 380mg

Spinach Shrimp Alfredo

Preparation time: 15 minutes

Cooking time: 20 minutes

Servings: 4

Ingredients

- 8 oz. fettuccine pasta
- 1 lb. shrimp, peeled and deveined
- 2 tbsp butter
- 3 cloves garlic, minced
- 1 cup of heavy cream
- 1 cup of grated Parmesan cheese
- 2 cups of fresh spinach leaves
- Salt and pepper as needed
- Fresh parsley, chopped (for garnish, optional)

Instructions

1. As directed on the package, prepare the fettuccine pasta until it is al dente. Drain, then set apart.
2. Melt the butter in a large pan over medium heat. After approximately a minute, add the minced garlic and simmer until fragrant.
3. When the shrimp are pink and cooked through, add them to the skillet and cook for 2-3 minutes on every side. Please remove the cooked shrimp from the skillet and lay them aside.
4. Lower the heat to low in the same skillet. Add the heavy cream, then gently boil the mixture.
5. Once the Parmesan cheese has melted and been thoroughly mixed into the cream sauce, stir in the cheese gradually. Stirring regularly, cook the sauce for 3 to 4 minutes or until it thickens.
6. Fresh spinach leaves are added and cooked for two to three minutes or until they wilt.
7. Then add the creamy spinach sauce to the pan with the cooked shrimp. As needed, add salt and pepper to the food.
8. Cooked fettuccine pasta should be added to the skillet and mixed with the creamy shrimp and spinach sauce.
9. If preferred, top the hot spinach shrimp Alfredo with freshly chopped parsley.

Nutrition Information (per serving)

Calories: 600 Protein: 40g Fat: 34g
Carbohydrates: 40g Fiber: 3g Sugar: 3g
Sodium: 680mg

Shrimp Scampi

Preparation time: 10 minutes

Cooking time: 10 minutes

Servings: 4

Ingredients

- 1 lb. large shrimp, peeled and deveined
- 8 oz. linguine or spaghetti
- 4 tbsp unsalted butter
- 4 cloves garlic, minced
- 1/2 cup of white wine.
- 2 tbsp fresh lemon juice
- 1/4 tsp red pepper flakes (adjust as needed)
- Salt and pepper as needed
- 2 tbsp chopped fresh parsley
- Lemon wedges for serving

Instructions

1. As directed on the package, prepare the linguine or spaghetti until it is al dente. Drain, then set apart.
2. Melt the butter in a large pan over medium heat. Add the minced garlic and cook until fragrant, about 1 minute.
3. When the shrimp are pink and cooked through, add them to the skillet and cook for 2-3 minutes on every side. From the skillet, take out the cooked shrimp and lay them aside.
4. Pour white wine into the skillet and deglaze it by scraping any browned pieces from the bottom with a spatula. For about 2 minutes, simmer to burn off the alcohol.
5. Red pepper flakes and lemon juice from a recent lemon are added. As needed, add salt and pepper to the food.
6. The tasty sauce should be added to the pan with the cooked shrimp.
7. Add the cooked linguine or spaghetti to the pan when the shrimp and sauce are thoroughly mixed.
8. Serve the shrimp scampi hot, topped with fresh parsley that has been cut, and with lemon wedges nearby to squeeze over the top.

Nutrition Information (per serving)

Calories: 390 Protein: 30g Fat: 13g
Carbohydrates: 34g Fiber: 2g Sugar: 1g
Sodium: 190mg

Fish Salad

Preparation time: 15 minutes

Cooking time: 10 minutes

Servings: 4

Ingredients

- 1 lb. white fish fillets.
- 4 cups of mixed salad greens
- 1 cucumber, thinly sliced
- 1 cup of cherry tomatoes, halved
- 1/4 red onion, thinly sliced
- 1/4 cup of Kalamata olives, pitted and halved
- 2 tbsp fresh lemon juice
- 2 tbsp olive oil
- 1 tbsp Dijon mustard
- Salt and pepper as needed
- Optional garnish: fresh herbs (such as dill or parsley)

Instructions

1. Preheat your oven to 375°F (190°C).
2. Arrange the white fish fillets on a baking sheet covered with aluminium foil or parchment paper. Add salt and pepper as needed.
3. The fish fillets should bake for about 10 minutes in the oven or until they are cooked and readily flake with a fork. Take them out of the oven, then let them cool a little.
4. Salad greens, cucumber slices, cherry tomatoes, red onion, and Kalamata olives should all be mixed in a big bowl.
5. Mix the fresh lemon juice, olive oil, Dijon mustard, salt, and pepper in a small bowl to make the dressing.
6. Add the cooked fish to the salad dish after breaking it into bite-sized pieces.

7. Toss the salad carefully to distribute the dressing over all ingredients evenly.
8. Top the fish salad with fresh herbs and divide it among serving dishes as desired.

Nutrition Information (per serving)

Calories: 220 Protein: 24g Fat: 10g Carbohydrates: 10g Fiber: 3g Sugar: 4g Sodium: 380mg

Flavorful Shrimp Scampi

Preparation time: 15 minutes

Cooking time: 10 minutes

Servings: 4

Ingredients

- 1 lb. large shrimp, peeled and deveined
- 8 oz. linguine or spaghetti
- 4 tbsp unsalted butter
- 4 cloves garlic, minced
- 1/2 cup of white wine
- 2 tbsp fresh lemon juice
- 1/4 tsp red pepper flakes (adjust as needed)
- Salt and pepper as needed
- 2 tbsp chopped fresh parsley
- Lemon wedges for serving

Instructions

1. As directed on the package, prepare the linguine or spaghetti until it is al dente. Drain, then set apart.
2. Melt the butter in a large pan over medium heat. Add the minced garlic and cook until fragrant, about 1 minute.
3. When the shrimp are pink and cooked through, add them to the skillet and cook for 2-3 minutes on every side. Please remove the cooked shrimp from the skillet and lay them aside.
4. Pour white wine into the skillet and deglaze it by scraping any browned pieces from the bottom with a spatula. For about 2 minutes, simmer to burn off the alcohol.
5. Red pepper flakes and lemon juice from a recent lemon are added. As needed, add salt and pepper to the food.
6. The tasty sauce should be added to the pan with the cooked shrimp.
7. Add the cooked linguine or spaghetti to the pan when the shrimp and sauce are thoroughly mixed.
8. Serve the shrimp scampi hot, topped with fresh parsley that has been cut, and with lemon wedges nearby to squeeze over the top.

Nutrition Information (per serving)

Calories: 390 Protein: 30g Fat: 13g Carbohydrates: 34g Fiber: 2g Sugar: 1g Sodium: 190mg

Creamy Tuna Salad

Preparation time: 10 minutes

Cooking time: 0 minutes

Servings: 4

Ingredients

- 2 cans (5 oz. every) tuna, drained
- 1/2 cup of mayonnaise
- 1/4 cup of Greek yogurt
- 2 tbsp lemon juice
- 1/4 cup of diced celery

- 1/4 cup of diced red onion
- 2 tbsp chopped fresh parsley
- 1/2 tsp Dijon mustard
- Salt and pepper as needed
- Optional additions: chopped pickles, diced tomatoes, sliced cucumber

Instructions

1. Tuna that has been drained, mayonnaise, Greek yogurt, lemon juice, sliced celery, diced red onion, chopped fresh parsley, Dijon mustard, salt, and pepper should all be mixed in a bowl.
2. Mix vigorously until the tuna salad is creamy and all the ingredients have been properly incorporated.
3. Taste the tuna salad and, if necessary, add more salt, pepper, or lemon juice to the seasoning.
4. Serve the creamy tuna salad over a bed of lettuce, in wraps, or atop sandwiches. Add extras like chopped pickles, diced tomatoes, or thinly sliced cucumber for additional flavor and crunch.

Nutrition Information (per serving)

Calories: 250 Protein: 20g Fat: 18g
Carbohydrates: 4g Fiber: 1g Sugar: 1g
Sodium: 380mg

Citrus Tilapia

Preparation time: 10 minutes

Cooking time: 15 minutes

Servings: 4

Ingredients

- 4 tilapia fillets (about 6 oz. every)
- 2 tbsp olive oil
- 2 cloves garlic, minced
- Zest and juice of 1 lemon
- Zest and juice of 1 orange
- 1 tsp dried thyme
- 1/2 tsp paprika
- Salt and pepper as needed
- Fresh parsley, chopped (for garnish, optional)

Instructions

1. Turn on the oven to 400 °F.
2. Put the tilapia fillets on a baking sheet with aluminium foil or parchment paper.
3. Olive oil, minced garlic, lemon and orange zests, lemon and orange juices, dried thyme, paprika, salt, and pepper are all mixed in a small bowl. To make a marinade for citrus, thoroughly stir.
4. The tilapia fillets should be well coated on both sides with the citrus marinade.
5. When tested with a fork, the tilapia should be baked in the oven for 12 to 15 minutes or until opaque and flaky.
6. Tilapia should be taken out of the oven and given time to rest.
7. If preferred, garnish the hot citrus tilapia with freshly chopped parsley.

Nutrition Information (per serving)

Calories: 200 Protein: 28g Fat: 9g
Carbohydrates: 2g Sugar: 1g

Lebanese-Style Cod Fillets

Preparation time: 15 minutes

Cooking time: 15 minutes

Servings: 4

Ingredients

- 4 cod fillets (about 6 oz. every)
- 2 tbsp olive oil
- 2 cloves garlic, minced
- 1 tsp ground cumin
- 1 tsp ground coriander
- 1/2 tsp paprika
- 1/2 tsp turmeric
- 1/4 tsp cinnamon
- Juice of 1 lemon
- Salt and pepper as needed
- Fresh parsley, chopped (for garnish, optional)

Instructions

1. Put the cod fillets on a baking sheet with aluminium foil or parchment paper.
2. Mix the olive oil, minced garlic, cumin, coriander, paprika, turmeric, cinnamon, lemon juice, salt, and pepper in a small bowl. To make a marinade, stir thoroughly.
3. Cod fillets should be well coated with the marinade and brushed on both sides.
4. When the fish is opaque and flakes readily with a fork, bake it in the oven for 12 to 15 minutes.
5. The fish should be taken out of the oven and rested.
6. If preferred, top the hot Lebanese-style cod fillets with freshly chopped parsley.

Nutrition Information (per serving)

Calories: 180 Protein: 24g Fat: 7g
Carbohydrates: 2g Fiber: 0g Sugar: 0g
Sodium: 80mg

Salmon Sage Bake

Preparation time: 10 minutes

Cooking time: 20 minutes

Servings: 4

Ingredients

- 4 salmon fillets (about 6 oz. every)
- 2 tbsp olive oil
- 2 tbsp fresh sage leaves, chopped
- 2 cloves garlic, minced
- Zest and juice of 1 lemon
- Salt and pepper as needed
- Lemon wedges for serving

Instructions

1. Preheat your oven to 400°F (200°C).
2. Put the salmon fillets on a baking sheet with aluminium foil or parchment paper.
3. Olive oil, minced garlic, lemon zest, lemon juice, salt, and pepper are all mixed in a small bowl with the chopped sage leaves. To make a sage marinade, stir thoroughly.
4. After being brushed over both sides, the salmon fillets should be well coated with the sage marinade.
5. The salmon should be baked in the oven for 15 to 20 minutes or until well-cooked and flakes readily with a fork.
6. The salmon should be taken out of the oven and rested.

7. Warm salmon sage bake should be served with lemon wedges for squeezing over the top.

Nutrition Information (per serving)

Calories: 300 Protein: 34g Fat: 16g Carbohydrates: 1g Fiber: 0g Sugar: 0g Sodium: 80mg

Pine Nut Haddock

Preparation time: 10 minutes

Cooking time: 15 minutes

Servings: 4

Ingredients

- 4 haddock fillets (about 6 oz. every)
- 1/4 cup of pine nuts
- 2 tbsp olive oil
- 2 cloves garlic, minced
- 1 tbsp fresh lemon juice
- 1 tsp lemon zest
- Salt and pepper as needed
- Fresh parsley, chopped (for garnish, optional)

Instructions

1. Preheat your oven to 400°F.
2. Haddock fillets should be on a baking pan covered with foil or parchment paper.
3. The pine nuts should be faintly brown after 2-3 minutes of medium heat toasting in a small pan. Heat has been removed; placed aside.
4. Olive oil, minced garlic, lemon juice, lemon zest, salt, and pepper should all be mixed in a small bowl. To produce a marinade, thoroughly stir.

5. Haddock fillets should be uniformly coated on both sides with the marinade.
6. Haddock fillets should be covered with toasted pine nuts, which you should gently press onto the surface of the fish.
7. Haddock should be baked in the preheated oven for 12-15 minutes or until it is well cooked and flakes readily when tested with a fork.
8. Haddock should be taken out of the oven and given time to rest.
9. If preferred, top the hot pine nut haddock with freshly chopped parsley.

Nutrition Information (per serving)

Calories: 260 Protein: 30g Fat: 14g Carbohydrates: 3g Fiber: 1g Sugar: 0g Sodium: 160mg

Catalán Salmon Tacos

Preparation time: 15 minutes

Cooking time: 15 minutes

Servings: 4

Ingredients

- 1 lb. salmon fillets, skin removed
- 8 small flour tortillas
- 1 cup of cherry tomatoes, halved
- 1/2 cup of red onion, thinly sliced
- 1/4 cup of fresh cilantro, chopped
- 1 tbsp olive oil
- 1 tbsp lemon juice
- 1 tsp smoked paprika
- 1/2 tsp ground cumin
- Salt and pepper as needed

- Optional toppings: sliced avocado, Greek yogurt or sour cream

Instructions

1. Turn on the oven to 400 °F.
2. Arrange the salmon fillets on a baking sheet covered with aluminium foil or parchment paper.
3. Mix the olive oil, lemon juice, smoked paprika, ground cumin, salt, and pepper in a small bowl.
4. The salmon fillets should be generously coated with the spice mixture by brushing it evenly.
5. For 12 to 15 minutes, or until the salmon is cooked through and flakes readily with a fork, bake the salmon in the preheated oven.
6. The salmon should be taken out of the oven and given time to cool. Use a fork to splinter the cooked salmon into manageable pieces.
7. The flour tortillas should be warmed in a microwave or a dry pan until they are flexible and soft.
8. Fill every tortilla with flakes of salmon, cherry tomatoes, red onion, and chopped cilantro to assemble the tacos.
9. If desired, drizzle the tacos with more lemon juice and olive oil.
10. Serve the Catalán salmon tacos hot and top with extras like sliced avocado and a dab of sour cream or Greek yogurt.

Nutrition Information (per serving, without toppings)

Calories: 340 Protein: 26g Fat: 13g
Carbohydrates: 30g Fiber: 3g Sugar: 4g
Sodium: 240mg

Salmon and Cauliflower Sheet Pan

Preparation time: 15 minutes

Cooking time: 25 minutes

Servings: 4

Ingredients

- 4 salmon fillets (about 6 oz. every)
- 1 small head of cauliflower
- 1 red bell pepper, sliced
- 1 yellow bell pepper, sliced
- 1 small red onion, sliced
- 2 tbsp olive oil
- 2 cloves garlic, minced
- 1 tsp smoked paprika
- 1/2 tsp dried thyme
- Salt and pepper as needed
- Lemon wedges for serving
- Fresh parsley, chopped (for garnish, optional)

Instructions

1. Preheat your oven to 425°F.
2. Cauliflower florets, bell pepper slices, and red onion slices should all be placed in a big bowl. Olive oil should be drizzled over the dish before adding salt, pepper, chopped garlic, smoky paprika, and dried thyme. Toss thoroughly to coat the veggies evenly.
3. On a large baking sheet, distribute the seasoned veggies in a single layer.
4. Along with the veggies on the baking sheet, arrange the salmon fillets. Salt and pepper the fish after drizzling it with a little olive oil.
5. For 20 to 25 minutes, or until the fish is cooked and the cauliflower is

soft and slightly caramelized, roast the salmon and cauliflower in the oven.

6. The sheet pan should be removed from the oven and allowed time to cool.

7. If preferred, sprinkle the salmon and cauliflower with freshly chopped parsley while still hot. Lemon wedges should be provided to squeeze over the fish.

Nutrition Information (per serving)

Calories: 360 Protein: 34g Fat: 18g
Carbohydrates: 14g Fiber: 5g Sugar: 6g
Sodium: 120mg

Spicy Trout Sheet Pan

Preparation time: 15 minutes

Cooking time: 20 minutes

Servings: 4

Ingredients

- 4 trout fillets (about 6 oz. every)
- 1 lb. baby potatoes, halved
- 1 cup of cherry tomatoes
- 1 red bell pepper, sliced
- 1 yellow bell pepper, sliced
- 1 small red onion, sliced
- 2 tbsp olive oil
- 2 tbsp lemon juice
- 1 tsp smoked paprika
- 1/2 tsp cayenne pepper (adjust as needed)
- 1/2 tsp dried thyme
- Salt and pepper as needed
- Fresh parsley, chopped (for garnish, optional)

Instructions

1. Preheat your oven to 425°F (220°C).

2. Baby potatoes cut in half, cherry tomatoes, bell peppers cut into slices, and red onion cut into slices should all be mixed in a big dish. Lemon juice and olive oil should be drizzled on. Add smoked paprika, cayenne, dried thyme, salt, and pepper as needed. Toss thoroughly to coat the veggies evenly.

3. On a large baking sheet, distribute the seasoned veggies in a single layer.

4. On the baking sheet, amidst the veggies, put the fish fillets. Salt and pepper the fish after drizzling it with a little olive oil.

5. For about 15 to 20 minutes, or until the potatoes are soft and the fish is cooked and flakes readily with a fork, roast the veggies and trout in the oven.

6. The sheet pan should be removed from the oven and allowed time to cool.

7. Garnish the hot, spicy fish and veggies with fresh, chopped parsley if preferred.

Nutrition Information (per serving)

Calories: 320 Protein: 30g Fat: 15g
Carbohydrates: 20g Fiber: 4g Sugar: 4g
Sodium: 80mg

Salmon Patties

Preparation time: 15 minutes

Cooking time: 10 minutes

Servings: 4

Ingredients

- 1 lb. canned salmon, drained and flaked
- 1/4 cup of bread crumbs
- 1/4 cup of finely chopped red onion
- 2 tbsp chopped fresh parsley
- 2 tbsp mayonnaise
- 1 tbsp Dijon mustard
- 1 egg, lightly beaten
- 1 tbsp lemon juice
- 1/2 tsp Old Bay seasoning (optional)
- Salt and pepper as needed
- 2 tbsp olive oil for cooking

Instructions

1. The tinned salmon, bread crumbs, red onion, parsley, mayonnaise, Dijon mustard, beaten egg, lemon juice, Old Bay seasoning (if used), salt, and pepper should all be mixed in a mixing bowl. All materials should be completely blended after mixing.
2. Create patties from the salmon mixture about 3 inches in diameter and 1/2 inch thick.
3. Over medium heat, warm the olive oil in a skillet.
4. The salmon patties should be golden brown and cooked through, so place them in a pan and cook for about 4-5 minutes on every side.
5. The salmon patties should be removed from the skillet and placed on a dish covered with paper towels to soak up any extra oil.
6. Serve the hot salmon patties with your preferred side dishes or as a sandwich on bread.

Nutrition Information

Calories: 280 Protein: 28g Fat: 16g
Carbohydrates: 7g Fiber: 1g Sugar: 1g
Sodium: 590mg

Spiced Eggplant Fritters

Preparation time: 20 minutes

Cooking time: 15 minutes

Servings: 4

Ingredients

- 1 large eggplant (about 1 lb.)
- 1/2 cup of chickpea flour
- 1/4 cup of finely chopped red onion
- 2 cloves garlic, minced
- 2 tbsp chopped fresh parsley
- 1 tsp ground cumin
- 1/2 tsp ground coriander
- 1/2 tsp paprika
- 1/4 tsp cayenne pepper (adjust as needed)
- Salt as need
- Vegetable oil for frying

Instructions

1. Put the cubed eggplant in a sieve after cutting it into tiny pieces. To remove any extra moisture, sprinkle with salt and let it rest for 10 minutes. The eggplant should be washed in cold water and dried with paper towels.

2. Chickpea flour, minced red onion, minced garlic, chopped parsley, ground cumin, ground coriander, paprika, cayenne pepper, and salt should all be mixed in a large mixing basin. To blend, thoroughly stir.
3. When the dried eggplant cubes are completely covered in the spice mixture, add them to the bowl.
4. In a skillet, heat vegetable oil over medium-low heat.
5. Shape a tiny fritter out of a tbsp of the eggplant mixture. Carefully put it into the heated oil. Avoid cramming the skillet with too much leftover mixture as you repeat the process.
6. The fritters should be fried for two to three minutes on every side or until crispy and golden.
7. Once cooked, move the fritters to a dish lined with paper towels to absorb extra oil.
8. The spicy eggplant fritters may be served hot as an appetizer or as a side dish with your preferred dipping sauce.

Nutrition Information

Calories: 130 Protein: 5g Fat: 5g
Carbohydrates: 18g Fiber: 6g Sugar: 3g
Sodium: 90mg

Broccoli Rice Casserole

Preparation time: 15 minutes

Cooking time: 35 minutes

Servings: 6

Ingredients

- 2 cups of broccoli florets
- 2 cups of cooked rice
- 1 cup of shredded cheddar cheese
- 1/2 cup of diced onion
- 1/2 cup of diced red bell pepper
- 1/2 cup of diced celery
- 1/2 cup of mayonnaise
- 1/2 cup of sour cream
- 2 tbsp melted butter
- 2 tbsp all-purpose flour
- 1 tsp garlic powder
- 1/2 tsp dried thyme
- Salt and pepper as needed
- Optional topping: crushed buttery crackers

Instructions

1. Set your oven's temperature to 350 °F (175 °C). Cooking or casserole utensils of 9x9 inches should be greased.
2. The broccoli florets should be blanched in a kettle of boiling water for two to three minutes to make them tender. Set aside after draining.
3. Cooked rice, grated cheddar cheese, chopped red bell pepper, diced celery, mayonnaise, sour cream, melted butter, flour, garlic powder, dried thyme, salt, and pepper should all be combined in a large mixing dish. To mix, thoroughly mix.

4. Broccoli florets that have been blanched should be included in the mixture by gently folding them.
5. After smoothing it out evenly, transfer the mixture to the oiled baking dish.
6. You may add a crispy topping to the dish by sprinkling crushed buttery crackers.
7. Until bubbling and the top is golden brown, bake the broccoli rice casserole in a preheated oven for 30-35 minutes.
8. Before serving, remove the casserole from the oven and allow it to cool for a while.

Nutrition Information

Calories: 340 Protein: 8g Fat: 22g
Carbohydrates: 29g Fiber: 2g Sugar: 3g
Sodium: 380mg

Grilled Eggplant and Tomato Pasta

Preparation time: 15 minutes

Cooking time: 25 minutes

Servings: 4

Ingredients

- 8 oz. pasta (such as penne or fusilli)
- 1 medium eggplant, sliced into rounds
- 2 large tomatoes, sliced
- 4 cloves garlic, minced
- 2 tbsp olive oil
- 1 tbsp balsamic vinegar
- 1/2 tsp dried basil
- 1/2 tsp dried oregano
- Salt and pepper as needed
- Grated Parmesan cheese for serving
- Fresh basil leaves, chopped (for garnish, optional)

Instructions

1. Preheat your grill or grill pan over medium heat.
2. As directed on the packaging, cook the pasta until it is al dente. Drain and reserve.
3. Brush the tomato and eggplant slices with olive oil as the pasta cooks.
4. Grill the tomato and eggplant slices on every side for 2 to 3 minutes until they are soft and have grill stains. Remove off the grill, then let them cool a little.
5. Cut the tomatoes and eggplant off the grill into bite-sized pieces.
6. Melt the olive oil in a large pan over medium heat. Once the garlic is aromatic, add it and simmer for approximately a minute.
7. Add the chopped tomatoes and eggplant to the skillet, and cook for 3–4 minutes or until cooked through.
8. Add salt, pepper, dried oregano, dry basil, and balsamic vinegar. To enable the flavors to mingle, cook for 2 to 3 minutes.
9. The grilled eggplant and tomato combination should blend well with the prepared pasta, which you should now add to the pan.
10. Serve the hot grilled eggplant and tomato spaghetti with grated Parmesan cheese and, if preferred, fresh chopped basil on top.

Nutrition Information (per serving)

Calories: 350 Protein: 10g Fat: 9g
Carbohydrates: 59g Fiber: 6g Sugar: 7g
Sodium: 110mg

Potato and Vegetable Casserole

Preparation time: 20 minutes

Cooking time: 45 minutes

Servings: 6

Ingredients

- 4 large potatoes, peeled and thinly sliced
- 1 medium onion, thinly sliced
- 2 cloves garlic, minced
- 2 carrots, peeled and thinly sliced
- 1 zucchini, thinly sliced
- 1 red bell pepper, thinly sliced
- 1 cup of broccoli florets
- 1 cup of cauliflower florets
- 1 cup of shredded cheddar cheese
- 1/4 cup of grated Parmesan cheese
- 1 cup of vegetable broth
- 1/4 cup of olive oil
- 1 tsp dried thyme
- 1/2 tsp dried rosemary
- Salt and pepper as needed
- Fresh parsley, chopped (for garnish, optional)

Instructions

1. Set your oven's temperature to 375°F (190°C). A 9x13-inch baking or casserole dish should be greased.
2. Sliced potatoes, onion, minced garlic, carrots, zucchini, red bell pepper, broccoli florets, and cauliflower florets should all be mixed in a big bowl. Well, mix the veggies by tossing.
3. Mix the vegetable broth, olive oil, salt, pepper, dried thyme, rosemary, and vegetable in a small bowl.
4. Arrange half of the vegetable mixture in layers in the oiled baking dish. The veggies should be covered with half the grated Parmesan cheese and half the shredded cheddar cheese.
5. Over the cheese and veggies, pour half of the vegetable broth mixture.
6. Repeat the layering with the remaining cheeses, veggies, and vegetable broth combination.
7. Bake in the oven for 30 minutes with the foil covering the baking dish.
8. Once the potatoes are cooked, and the cheese is brown and bubbling, remove the cover and bake for another 15 minutes.
9. After taking the casserole out of the oven, give it some time to cool.
10. Top the hot potato and vegetable casserole with freshly chopped parsley before serving.

Nutrition Information (per serving, based on 6 servings)

Calories: 290 Protein: 9g Fat: 14g
Carbohydrates: 34g Fiber: 5g Sugar: 4g
Sodium: 380mg

Cereal Bowl with Cashew and Tahini Sauce

Preparation time: 10 minutes

Cooking time: 0 minutes

Servings: 1

Ingredients

- 1 cup of your favourite cereal or granola
- 1 ripe banana, sliced
- 1/4 cup of fresh berries (such as blueberries, strawberries, or raspberries)
- 1 tbsp cashews, chopped
- 1 tbsp hemp seeds (optional)
- 1 tbsp chia seeds (optional)
- For the Cashew and Tahini Sauce:
- 2 tbsp cashew butter
- 1 tbsp tahini
- 1 tbsp maple syrup or honey
- 1/2 tsp vanilla extract
- 2-3 tbsp almond milk (or any other plant-based milk), as needed for desired consistency

Instructions

1. Put your favourite cereal or nuts in the bottom of a bowl.
2. Slice the banana and put the fresh berries on top of the rice.
3. Add chopped peanuts, hemp seeds (if you want to use them), and chia seeds (if you want to use them).
4. To make the cashew and tahini sauce, mix the cashew butter, tahini, maple syrup or honey, and vanilla flavor in a small bowl.
5. Whisking constantly, slowly add almond milk to the sauce mixture until it is the right consistency to pour.
6. Pour the sauce made from cashews and tahini over the cereal.
7. Enjoy your healthy and tasty bowl of cereal with cashew and tahini sauce.

Nutrition Information (per serving)

Calories: 450 Protein: 10g Fat: 24g Carbohydrates: 52g Fiber: 8g Sugar: 22g Sodium: 60mg

Creamy Zucchini and Potato Soup

Preparation time: 15 minutes

Cooking time: 25 minutes

Servings: 4

Ingredients

- 2 medium zucchini, chopped
- 2 medium potatoes, peeled and chopped
- 1 small onion, chopped
- 2 cloves garlic, minced
- 4 cups of vegetable broth
- 1 cup of unsweetened almond milk
- 2 tbsp olive oil
- 1 tsp dried thyme
- 1/2 tsp dried rosemary
- Salt and pepper as needed
- Fresh parsley, chopped (for garnish, optional)

Instructions

1. Olive oil should be heated in a sizable pot over medium heat. Sauté the minced garlic and diced onion

for 3–4 minutes or until fragrant and softening.

2. Cubed potatoes and zucchini should be added to the saucepan, salt, pepper, dried thyme, and rosemary. The spices should be thoroughly mixed in and coated on the vegetables.

3. Bring the mixture to a boil after adding the veggie broth. The potatoes and zucchini should be soft after 15 to 20 minutes of simmering on low heat with the lid on.

4. Blend the soup with an immersion or standard blender until it is smooth and creamy. Blend the soup in batches using a conventional blender; be careful because it will be hot.

5. Put the soup back in the pot and add the almond milk if required. Stirring occasionally, cook the soup over low heat for 5 minutes or until thoroughly heated.

6. If necessary, add more salt and pepper after tasting the food.

7. If desired, top the hot, creamy soup with fresh chopped parsley. It is made with zucchini and potatoes.

Nutrition Information (per serving)

Calories: 180 Protein: 4g Fat: 8g
Carbohydrates: 26g Fiber: 4g Sugar: 4g
Sodium: 560mg

Vegan Ratatouille

Preparation time: 15 minutes

Cooking time: 45 minutes

Servings: 4

Ingredients

- 1 eggplant, diced
- 2 zucchinis, diced
- 1 yellow bell pepper, diced
- 1 red bell pepper, diced
- 1 onion, diced
- 3 cloves garlic, minced
- 2 tomatoes, diced
- 2 tbsp tomato paste
- 2 tbsp olive oil
- 1 tsp dried thyme
- 1 tsp dried oregano
- Salt and pepper as needed
- Fresh basil leaves, chopped (for garnish, optional)

Instructions

1. Preheat your oven to 375°F.
2. Melt the olive oil in a large skillet over medium heat. Add the diced onion and minced garlic, and cook for 3–4 minutes or until aromatic and softening.
3. The skillet should now contain the diced eggplant, zucchini, and yellow and red bell peppers. The vegetables should be tender after 5 minutes of sautéing with intermittent stirring.
4. Add salt, pepper, dried thyme, oregano, chopped tomatoes, tomato paste, and salt and pepper as needed. To blend, thoroughly mash.
5. Transfer the mixture to a baking dish from the skillet.

6. Bake the baking dish for 30 minutes in a preheated oven with the foil covering.
7. After removing the foil, the vegetables should be fully cooked and soft after another 10-15 minutes of baking.
8. After taking the ratatouille out of the oven, give it some time to cool.
9. Top the hot vegan ratatouille with freshly chopped basil before serving.

Nutrition Information (per serving)

Calories: 140 Protein: 4g Fat: 7g
Carbohydrates: 20g Fiber: 7g Sugar: 11g
Sodium: 350mg

CHAPTER 6: SMOOTHIE AND JUICE

Jalapeño and Cilantro Juice

Preparation time: 10 minutes

Cooking time: 0 minutes

Servings: 2

Ingredients

- 2 jalapeño peppers, seeds removed (adjust quantity based on the desired spiciness)
- 1 cup of fresh cilantro leaves
- 1 lime, juiced
- 1 tbsp honey or maple syrup (optional for sweetness)
- 1 cup of water
- Ice cubes (optional)

Instructions

1. Mix the jalapenos, cilantro, lime juice, honey, or maple syrup (if using), and water in a blender or food processor.
2. When the mixture is smooth, and the components are thoroughly blended, blend at a high speed.
3. Add extra honey, maple syrup, or cilantro to the juice after tasting it to modify the flavor.
4. Filter the juice to remove any solids using a fine-mesh screen.
5. Serve the cooled jalapeno and cilantro juice. For a cool beverage, you can add ice cubes.

Nutrition Information (per serving)

Calories: 25 Protein: 0.5g Fat: 0.3g
Carbohydrates: 6g Fiber: 1g Sugar: 3g
Sodium: 5mg

Grape Weight Loss Juice

Preparation time: 10 minutes

Cooking time: 0 minutes

Servings: 2

Ingredients

- 2 cups of seedless grapes (any variety)
- 1 medium cucumber, peeled and chopped
- 1 lemon, juiced
- 1-inch piece of fresh ginger peeled
- 1 cup of spinach leaves
- 1 cup of water
- Ice cubes (optional)

Instructions

1. The seedless grapes, cucumber chunks, lemon juice, ginger, spinach leaves, and water should all be mixed in a blender or juicer.
2. Blend quickly until the mixture is smooth and all the components are well incorporated.
3. You can pass the juice through a fine-mesh sieve if you choose to get rid of any solids.
4. The grape weight loss juice should be served cold. For a cooling beverage, add ice cubes.

Nutrition Information (per serving)

Calories: 90 Protein: 1g Fat: 0.4g
Carbohydrates: 22g Fiber: 2g Sugar: 16g
Sodium: 10mg

Icy Orange Juice with Lemon

Preparation time: 10 minutes

Cooking time: 0 minutes

Servings: 2

Ingredients

- 4 oranges
- 1 lemon
- Ice cubes

Instructions

1. Remove any seeds before squeezing the orange and lemon juice into a dish or pitcher.
2. Juice from freshly squeezed lemon and oranges should be added to a blender.
3. A few ice cubes should be added to the mixer.

4. Blend at high speed only until the mixture comes together and becomes foamy.
5. If necessary, add extra lemon juice after tasting the juice to your preferred taste.
6. Serve the cold orange juice with lemon right away in ice-filled cups.

Nutrition Information (per serving)

Calories: 100 Protein: 2g Fat: 0.5g
Carbohydrates: 24g Fiber: 5g Sugar: 18g
Sodium: 0mg

Fruity Mixed Juice

Preparation time: 10 minutes

Cooking time: 0 minutes

Servings: 2

Ingredients

- 1 medium apple, cored and chopped
- 1 medium pear, cored and chopped
- 1 cup of strawberries, hulled and halved
- 1 cup of pineapple chunks
- 1 cup of watermelon chunks
- 1/2 cup of orange juice (freshly squeezed if possible)
- Ice cubes

Instructions

1. All fruits should be washed, prepared, corked, chopped, and hulled.
2. Mix the strawberries, pineapple pieces, watermelon chunks, pear chunks, and orange juice in a blender or juicer.

3. Blend quickly until the mixture is smooth and the components are well blended.
4. Filter the juice to remove any solids using a fine-mesh screen.
5. Immediately serve the fruity blended juice in ice-filled cups.

Nutrition Information (per serving)

Calories: 120 Protein: 2g Fat: 0.5g
Carbohydrates: 30g Fiber: 5g Sugar: 22g
Sodium: 5mg

Avocado Mix with Ice

Preparation time: 10 minutes

Cooking time: 0 minutes

Servings: 2

Ingredients

- 1 ripe avocado
- 1 cup of milk (dairy or plant-based)
- 2 tbsp honey or maple syrup
- 1 tsp vanilla extract
- Ice cubes

Instructions

1. Remove the avocado's pit, cut it in half, then scoop the flesh into a blender.
2. Blender ingredients for milk, honey or maple syrup, and vanilla extract.
3. Blend at high speed just until the mixture becomes creamy and smooth.
4. Add extra honey or maple syrup after tasting the avocado mixture to adjust its sweetness if necessary.

5. Blend the mixture again while adding ice cubes to make it slushy and foamy.
6. Serve the avocado mixture immediately after pouring it into glasses with ice.

Nutrition Information (per serving)

Calories: 230 Protein: 3g Fat: 14g
Carbohydrates: 25g Fiber: 7g Sugar: 16g
Sodium: 40mg

Apple-Carrot Juice

Preparation time: 10 minutes

Cooking time: 0 minutes

Servings: 2

Ingredients

- 2 medium apples
- 4 medium carrots
- 1/2 lemon, juiced
- 1-inch piece of fresh ginger (optional for added flavor)
- Ice cubes (optional)

Instructions

1. The apples and carrots should be cleaned and prepared by coring, peeling (if desired), and slicing them into small pieces.
2. Peel and chop whatever ginger you use into small pieces.
3. The diced apples, carrots, lemon juice, and ginger (if used) should all be placed in a juicer or blender. You should add a little water to your blender to make mixing easier.

4. Until the ingredients are well-mixed and smooth, blend or juice them.
5. You can pass the juice through a fine-mesh sieve if you choose to get rid of any solids.
6. If preferred, immediately serve the apple-carrot juice in glasses with ice cubes.

Nutrition Information (per serving)

Calories: 120 Protein: 1g Fat: 0g
Carbohydrates: 30g Fiber: 7g Sugar: 21g
Sodium: 80mg

Kale-Banana Smoothie

Preparation time: 5 minutes

Cooking time: 0 minutes

Servings: 1

Ingredients

- 1 cup of kale leaves, stems removed
- 1 ripe banana
- 1/2 cup of almond milk (or any other plant-based milk)
- 1 tbsp nut butter (such as almond butter or peanut butter)
- 1 tbsp chia seeds
- 1/2 tsp honey or maple syrup
- Ice cubes (optional)

Instructions

1. Remove the stems from the kale leaves and give them a good wash.
2. The banana is ripe; peel and cut it.
3. Put the kale leaves, banana slices, almond milk, nut butter, chia seeds, and honey or maple syrup (if using) in a blender.

4. Blend at high speed just until the mixture becomes creamy and smooth.
5. If desired, put ice cubes in the blender and blitz the mixture once more until it is cooled and foamy.
6. Serve the kale-banana smoothie right away by pouring it into a glass.

Nutrition Information (per serving)

Calories: 250 Protein: 7g Fat: 11g
Carbohydrates: 34g Fiber: 9g Sugar: 15g
Sodium: 120mg

Apple Tart Smoothie

Preparation time: 10 minutes

Cooking time: 0 minutes

Servings: 2

Ingredients

- 2 medium apples, cored and chopped
- 1 ripe banana
- 1/2 cup of plain Greek yogurt
- 1/2 cup of unsweetened almond milk
- 1 tbsp almond butter or peanut butter
- 1 tsp ground cinnamon
- 1/2 tsp vanilla extract
- 1 tbsp honey or maple syrup (optional for added sweetness)
- Ice cubes (optional)

Instructions

1. The apples should be washed, cored, and chopped.
2. Slice and peel the ripe banana.

3. Chop the apples, slice the banana, and add the Greek yogurt, almond milk, almond butter (or peanut butter), cinnamon, vanilla extract, honey, and maple syrup (if used) to a blender.
4. The mixture should be smooth and creamy after a high-speed blend.
5. Add ice to the blender and reprocess until the smoothie is cold and foamy.
6. Immediately serve the apple tart smoothie by pouring it into glasses.

Nutrition Information (per serving)

Calories: 220 Protein: 6g Fat: 7g
Carbohydrates: 38g Fiber: 6g Sugar: 24g
Sodium: 80mg

Kiwi, Zucchini, and Pear Smoothie

Preparation time: 10 minutes

Cooking time: 0 minutes

Servings: 2

Ingredients

- 2 ripe kiwis, peeled and sliced
- 1 small zucchini, chopped
- 1 ripe pear, cored and chopped
- 1 cup of spinach leaves
- 1 cup of unsweetened almond milk (or any other plant-based milk)
- 1 tbsp chia seeds
- 1 tbsp honey or maple syrup (optional for added sweetness)
- Ice cubes (optional)

Instructions

1. Peeling and slicing the kiwis will prepare them after washing.
2. The zucchini should be cut into tiny pieces.
3. Slice and core the pears.
4. Blend the sliced kiwis, diced zucchini, diced pear, spinach leaves, almond milk, chia seeds, and honey or maple syrup (if using) in a food processor or blender.
5. The mixture should be smooth and creamy after a high-speed blend.
6. Add ice to the blender and reprocess until the smoothie is cold and foamy.
7. Serve the kiwi, zucchini, and pear smoothie right away after pouring it into glasses.

Nutrition Information (per serving)

Calories: 150 Protein: 4g Fat: 3g
Carbohydrates: 30g Fiber: 7g Sugar: 18g
Sodium: 80mg

Green Mango Smoothie

Preparation time: 10 minutes

Cooking time: 0 minutes

Servings: 2

Ingredients

- 1 green mango, peeled and sliced
- 1 ripe banana
- 1 cup of spinach leaves
- 1/2 cup of Greek yogurt (or dairy-free alternative)
- 1/2 cup of unsweetened almond milk (or any other plant-based milk)
- 1 tbsp honey or maple syrup (optional for added sweetness)

- 1 tbsp chia seeds
- Ice cubes (optional)

Instructions

1. Slice and peel the green mango.
2. Slice and peel the ripe banana.
3. Put the spinach leaves, Greek yogurt, almond milk, honey or maple syrup (if using), chia seeds, and the green mango and banana slices in a blender.
4. The mixture should be smooth and creamy after a high-speed blend.
5. Add ice to the blender and reprocess until the smoothie is cold and foamy.
6. Pour the smoothie made with green mango into glasses, then serve immediately.

Nutrition Information (per serving)

Calories: 180 Protein: 7g Fat: 3g Carbohydrates: 36g Fiber: 5g Sugar: 25g Sodium: 60mg

Carrot-Orange-Ginger Juice

Preparation Time: 10 minutes

Cooking Time: N/A

Total Time: 10 minutes

Ingredients

- 4 medium-sized carrots
- 2 large oranges
- 1-inch piece of fresh ginger

Instructions

1. Peel and wash the ginger, oranges, and carrots.
2. Oranges and carrots should be cut into tiny bits.
3. Cut the ginger root into smaller pieces.
4. Use a juicer or blender to mix all the ingredients.
5. Juice or blend the mixture until it has a smooth consistency.
6. If using a blender, filter the juice to remove any pulp using a fine-mesh sieve or cheesecloth.
7. Serve the juice right away by pouring it into a glass.

Nutrition Information (per serving)

Calories: 120 Carbohydrates: 28g Protein: 2g Fat: 1g Fiber: 6g

Green Detox Juice

Preparation Time: 10 minutes

Cooking Time: N/A

Total Time: 10 minutes

Ingredients

- 2 cups of fresh spinach leaves
- 1 medium cucumber
- 2 stalks celery
- 1 green apple
- 1 lemon

Instructions

1. Thoroughly clean all the components.
2. Smaller the bits of cucumber, celery, green apple, and lemon.
3. Mix the spinach leaves and chopped ingredients in a juicer or blender.

4. Juice or blend until well blended and smooth.
5. If using a blender, filter the juice to remove any pulp using a fine-mesh sieve or cheesecloth.
6. Serve the juice right away by pouring it into a glass.

Nutrition Information (per serving)

Calories: 100 Carbohydrates: 24g Protein: 4g Fat: 1g Fiber: 8g

Pineapple-Ginger Morning

Preparation Time: 15 minutes

Cooking Time: N/A

Total Time: 15 minutes

Ingredients

- 1 small pineapple
- 2 apples
- 1-inch piece of fresh ginger
- 1 tbsp lemon juice

Instructions

1. Cut the pineapple into smaller pieces after peeling.
2. Apples should be cored and cut into smaller pieces.
3. Ginger should be peeled and cut into smaller pieces.
4. Mix the pineapple, apples, ginger, and lemon juice with a juicer or blender.
5. Juice or blend until well blended and smooth.
6. If using a blender, filter the juice to remove any pulp using a fine-mesh sieve or cheesecloth.
7. Serve the juice right away by pouring it into a glass.

Nutrition Information (per serving)

Calories: 180 Carbohydrates: 46g Protein: 1g Fat: 0g Fiber: 6g

Citrus-Berry Morning Juice

Preparation Time: 10 minutes

Cooking Time: N/A

Total Time: 10 minutes

Ingredients

- 2 oranges
- 1 grapefruit
- 1 cup of mixed berries
- 1 tbsp honey (optional for added sweetness)

Instructions

1. Remove the pith and outer skin from the oranges and grapefruit before peeling.
2. Oranges and grapefruit should be cut into smaller pieces.
3. The mixed berries should be cleaned.
4. Put the berries and citrus fruits in a juicer or blender.
5. Juice or blend until well blended and smooth.
6. If using a blender, filter the juice to remove any pulp using a fine-mesh sieve or cheesecloth.
7. If desired, add honey and thoroughly stir.
8. Serve the juice right away by pouring it into a glass.

Nutrition Information (per serving)

Calories: 150 Carbohydrates: 36g Protein: 3g Fat: 0g Fiber: 8g

CHAPTER 7: DESSERT

Apricot Crisp

Preparation Time: 15 minutes

Cooking Time: 40 minutes

Total Time: 55 minutes

Ingredients

- 8-10 fresh apricots, pitted and sliced
- 1 tbsp lemon juice
- 1/4 cup of granulated sugar
- 1/2 tsp vanilla extract
- For the Crisp Topping:
- 3/4 cup of old-fashioned rolled oats
- 1/2 cup of all-purpose flour
- 1/2 cup of packed brown sugar
- 1/4 tsp salt
- 1/2 tsp ground cinnamon
- 1/3 cup of cold unsalted butter, cut into small pieces

Instructions

1. Preheat your oven to 375°F and grease a baking dish.
2. Mix the sliced apricots, lemon juice, sugar, and vanilla extract in a bowl. Toss the apricots until they are well covered. Let it sit for 5 minutes.
3. Mix the rolling oats, all-purpose flour, brown sugar, salt, and cinnamon powder in a separate bowl.
4. Mix the cold pieces of butter into the oats. Mix the butter with your

hands or a pastry cutter until it resembles small bits.
5. Put the fruit mixture into the baking dish that has been oiled.
6. Spread the oat mixture out over the plums in an even layer.
7. Bake for about 35-40 minutes in an oven that has already been warm or until the topping is golden brown and the apricots are soft.
8. Take it out of the oven and wait a few minutes before serving.
9. Warm the apricot crisp and top with vanilla ice cream or whipped cream.

Nutrition Information (per serving)

Calories: 250 Carbohydrates: 44g Protein: 3g Fat: 9g Fiber: 3g

Baked Apples with Almonds

Preparation Time: 15 minutes

Cooking Time: 30 minutes

Total Time: 45 minutes

Ingredients

- 4 medium-sized apples (such as Granny Smith or Honeycrisp)
- 1/4 cup of chopped almonds
- 2 tbsp honey or maple syrup
- 1 tsp ground cinnamon
- 1/4 tsp ground nutmeg
- 1 tbsp unsalted butter, melted
- Optional toppings: Greek yogurt, vanilla ice cream, or caramel sauce

Instructions

1. Preheat your oven to 375°F (190°C).

2. Wash and pat dry the apples. Cut the top off every apple and remove the core to make a hole.
3. Put the chopped nuts, honey or maple syrup, ground cinnamon, ground nutmeg, and melted butter in a small bowl and mix well. Blend well.
4. Put some of the nut paste into every apple and gently press down.
5. Place the stuffed apples in a baking dish and drizzle any leftover nut mixture on top.
6. Bake for about 25 to 30 minutes in an oven that has been heated until the apples are soft, and the almond topping is golden brown.
7. Take the apples out of the oven and let them cool for a few minutes.
8. Serve the baked apples hot, with Greek yogurt, vanilla ice cream, or caramel sauce on top.

Nutrition Information (per serving)

Calories: 200 Carbohydrates: 34g Protein: 3g Fat: 8g Fiber: 5g

Berries with Balsamic Vinegar

Preparation Time: 5 minutes

Cooking Time: 0 minutes

Total Time: 5 minutes

Ingredients

- 2 cups of mixed fresh berries
- 1 tbsp balsamic vinegar
- 1 tbsp honey or maple syrup
- Fresh mint leaves for garnish (optional)

Instructions

1. Rinse the berries with cold water and dry them with a paper towel. If you want to use strawberries, cut them in half or quarters and remove the tops.
2. Mix the berries, balsamic vinegar, and honey or maple syrup in a bowl. Mix gently so that all of the berries get covered.
3. Let the berries soak in the mixture for a few minutes so the tastes can mix.
4. Pour any leftover vinegar mixture over the berries and serve them in bowls or plates.
5. Add fresh mint leaves as a garnish to make it look and taste even better.
6. Right away, eat the berries with balsamic vinegar.

Nutrition Information (per serving)

Calories: 80 Carbohydrates: 20g Protein: 1g Fat: 0g Fiber: 4g

Cookie Cream Shake

Preparation Time: 5 minutes

Cooking Time: 0 minutes

Total Time: 5 minutes

Ingredients

- 2 cups of vanilla ice cream
- 1 cup of milk (any type)
- 4-6 chocolate sandwich cookies (such as Oreos)
- 1/2 tsp vanilla extract
- Whipped cream for topping (optional)

- Crushed cookies for garnish (optional)

Instructions

1. Put the vanilla ice cream, milk, chocolate sandwich cookies, and vanilla extract in a blender and mix until smooth.
2. Blend quickly until the ingredients are well mixed and the shake is smooth and creamy.
3. If you want the consistency to be thinner or the taste of the cookies to be stronger, you can add more milk or cookies.
4. The shake is poured into cups.
5. If you want, you can put whipped cream and crushed cookies on top.
6. Use a straw or a spoon to serve the Cookie Cream Shake immediately.

Nutrition Information (per serving)

Calories: 400 Carbohydrates: 50g Protein: 8g Fat: 20g Fiber: 1g

Yogurt Cheesecake

Preparation Time: 20 minutes

Cooking Time: 1 hour 10 minutes

Chilling Time: 4 hours or overnight

Total Time: 5 hours 30 minutes

Ingredients

For the Crust

- 1/4 cup of unsalted butter, melted
- 2 tbsp granulated sugar

1 1/2 cups of graham cracker crumbs

For the Filling:

- 24 oz (680g) cream cheese, softened
- 1 cup of Greek yogurt
- 1 cup of granulated sugar
- 3 large eggs
- 1 tsp vanilla extract
- Zest of 1 lemon
- 2 tbsp all-purpose flour

Instructions

1. Preheat your oven to 325°F (160°C).
2. Mix the melted butter, crushed graham crackers, and granulated sugar for the crust in a bowl. Mix just enough to coat the crumbs all over.
3. Press the crumbs mixture in the bottom of a 9-inch (23-cm) spring form pan. Press the crumbs down firmly using the back of a spoon or the base of a glass.
4. Cream the cream cheese in a large mixing bowl until it is smooth and creamy.
5. The cream cheese is mixed with Greek yogurt, sugar, eggs, vanilla, lemon zest, and flour. Blend everything well and thoroughly until the mixture is smooth.
6. Over the spring form pan's crust, pour the filling.
7. Use a spatula or the back of a spoon to level the top.
8. Put a baking sheet below the spring form pan to catch any potential spills.
9. Bake the cheesecake for 1 hour and 10 minutes until the edges are set but the center is still jiggly.
10. To prevent breaking, turn off the oven and let the cheesecake inside for an hour.

11. The cheesecake should be removed from the oven and cooled entirely on a wire rack.
12. Once the cheesecake has cooled, please place it in the refrigerator for at least 4 hours or overnight to enable it to set.
13. Serve chilled, and enjoy!

Nutrition Information (per serving, based on 12 servings)

Calories: 370 Carbohydrates: 29g Protein: 8g Fat: 25g Fiber: 0g

Pumpkin Pie

Preparation Time: 20 minutes

Cooking Time: 1 hour 10 minutes

Total Time: 1 hour 30 minutes

Ingredients

- 1 3/4 cups of pumpkin puree
- 3/4 cup of granulated sugar
- 1 cup of evaporated milk
- 2 large eggs
- 1 tsp vanilla extract
- 1 tsp ground cinnamon
- 1/2 tsp ground ginger
- 1/4 tsp ground nutmeg
- 1/4 tsp ground cloves
- 1/4 tsp salt
- 1 unbaked 9-inch pie crust

Instructions

1. Preheat your oven to 425°F (220°C).
2. Mix the pumpkin puree, sugar, evaporated milk, eggs, vanilla extract, cinnamon, ginger, nutmeg, cloves, and salt in a large mixing bowl. Mix well until all of the ingredients are well blended.
3. Pour the pumpkin filling into the unbaked pie crust. Use a spatula or the back of a spoon to smooth the top.
4. Bake in an oven that has already been heated for 15 minutes. Then, turn the oven to 350°F (175°C) and bake for another 55 minutes, or until the filling is set and a knife put in the middle comes out clean.
5. Take the pie out of the oven and set it on a wire rack to cool fully.
6. Once the pie has cooled, please put it in the fridge for at least 2 hours before serving it so it can set and get hard.
7. Slice the pumpkin pie and serve it cold. You can top it with whipped cream or spice if you like.

Nutrition Information

Calories: 280 Carbohydrates: 45g Protein: 6g Fat: 9g

Sweet Potato Pie

Preparation Time: 30 minutes

Cooking Time: 1 hour

Total Time: 1 hour 30 minutes

Ingredients

- 2 cups of cooked and mashed sweet potatoes
- 3/4 cup of granulated sugar
- 1/2 cup of milk (any type)
- 2 large eggs
- 2 tbsp melted unsalted butter
- 1 tsp vanilla extract
- 1/2 tsp ground cinnamon
- 1/4 tsp ground nutmeg

- 1/4 tsp salt
- 1 unbaked 9-inch pie crust

Instructions

1. Preheat your oven to 350°F (175°C).
2. Mix the mashed sweet potatoes, sugar, milk, eggs, melted butter, vanilla extract, cinnamon, nutmeg, and salt in a big mixing bowl. Mix well until all of the ingredients are well blended.
3. Pour the sweet potato filling into the unbaked pie crust and smooth the top with a spatula or the back of a spoon.
4. Bake in an oven that has already been warm for about an hour or until the filling is set and a toothpick stuck in the middle comes out clean.
5. Take the pie out of the oven and set it on a wire rack to cool fully.
6. Once the pie has cooled, please put it in the fridge for at least 2 hours before serving it so it can set and get hard.
7. Cut the sweet potato pie into pieces and serve it cold. You can top it with whipped cream or cinnamon if you like.

Nutrition Information

Calories: 280 Carbohydrates: 47g Protein: 4g Fat: 9g Fiber: 2g

Apple-Berry Cobbler

Preparation Time: 20 minutes

Cooking Time: 40 minutes

Total Time: 1 hour

Ingredients

For the Fruit Filling

- 4 cups of peeled, cored, and sliced apples (such as Granny Smith or Honeycrisp)
- 2 cups of mixed berries (such as blueberries, raspberries, or blackberries)
- 1/2 cup of granulated sugar
- 2 tbsp all-purpose flour
- 1 tbsp lemon juice
- 1 tsp vanilla extract
- 1/2 tsp ground cinnamon

For the Cobbler Topping:

- 1 cup of all-purpose flour
- 1/4 cup of granulated sugar
- 1 tsp baking powder
- 1/4 tsp salt
- 1/4 cup of cold unsalted butter, cut into small pieces
- 1/4 cup of milk (any type)
- 1 tsp vanilla extract

Instructions

1. Preheat your oven to 375°F (190°C).
2. Mix the sliced apples, mixed berries, granulated sugar, all-purpose flour, lemon juice, vanilla extract, and ground cinnamon in a big bowl for the fruit filling. Mix gently until all of the fruit is covered. Let it sit for a few minutes so that the tastes can mix.

3. Put the fruit filling in a baking dish or a pan made of cast iron.
4. Mix the all-purpose flour, sugar, baking powder, and salt in a separate bowl for the cobbler topping.
5. Mix the cold pieces of butter into the flour. Cut the butter into the flour with a pastry cutter or your fingers until it looks like coarse bits.
6. Add the milk and vanilla extract and stir until they are mixed in. Make sure to mix only a little.
7. Put spoonfuls of the cobbler topping on top of the fruit filling in an even layer.
8. Bake for about 40 minutes in an oven that has already been warmed or until the fruit is boiling and the topping is golden brown.
9. Take it out of the oven and wait a few minutes before serving.
10. Serve the warm apple-berry pie with vanilla ice cream or whipped cream.

Nutrition Information

Calories: 280 Carbohydrates: 57g Protein: 3g Fat: 7g Fiber: 5g

Mint Chocolate Dessert with Banana

Preparation Time: 10 minutes

Cooking Time: 0 minutes

Chilling Time: 2 hours

Total Time: 2 hours 10 minutes

Ingredients

- 2 ripe bananas, sliced

- 1 cup of Greek yogurt
- 1 tbsp honey or maple syrup
- 1/2 tsp peppermint extract
- 1/4 cup of dark chocolate chips, melted
- Fresh mint leaves for garnish (optional)

Instructions

1. Blend or process the Greek yogurt, honey or maple syrup, and peppermint flavor in a mixer or food processor. Mix until everything is smooth and well-mixed.
2. Stack the banana slices and the mint-flavored Greek yogurt mixture in glasses or bowls.
3. Repeat the stages until you've used all ingredients, ending with the yogurt mixture.
4. Pour the dark chocolate that has been melted over every treat.
5. If you want, you can decorate with fresh mint leaves.
6. Cover the treats and put them in the fridge for at least 2 hours to set and get cold.
7. Serve the Mint Chocolate Dessert with Banana cold, and enjoy!

Nutrition Information (per serving, based on 2 servings)

Calories: 220 Carbohydrates: 38g Protein: 11g Fat: 5g Fiber: 4g

Baked Apples with Cherries and Almonds

Preparation Time: 15 minutes

Cooking Time: 40 minutes

Total Time: 55 minutes

Ingredients

- 4 medium-sized apples (such as Granny Smith or Honeycrisp)
- 1/2 cup of dried cherries
- 1/4 cup of chopped almonds
- 2 tbsp honey or maple syrup
- 1 tsp ground cinnamon
- 1/4 tsp ground nutmeg
- 1 tbsp unsalted butter, melted

Instructions

1. Set your oven to 375°F (190°C) and grease a baking dish.
2. Core the apples to make a hole in the middle. You can keep the bottom whole so that it can hold the filling.
3. Put the dried cherries, chopped almonds, honey or maple syrup, cinnamon powder, nutmeg powder, and melted butter into a bowl. Blend well.
4. Put some of the cherry and nut paste into every apple and gently press it down.
5. Put the apples that have been stuffed in the oiled baking dish.
6. Pour the cherry and nut mixture on top of the apples if there is any leftover.
7. Bake in an oven that has already been hot for about 35 to 40 minutes or until the apples are soft and the sauce has become caramelized.
8. Take the apples out of the oven and let them cool for a few minutes.
9. If you like, serve the Baked Apples with Cherries and Almonds warm, with vanilla ice cream or whipped cream.

Nutrition Information (per serving)

Calories: 230 Carbohydrates: 46g Protein: 3g Fat: 6g Fiber: 6g

Fruit Cake

Preparation Time: 30 minutes

Cooking Time: 2 hours 30 minutes

Total Time: 3 hours

Ingredients

- 2 cups of mixed dried fruits
- 1 cup of chopped nuts
- 1 cup of unsalted butter, softened
- 1 cup of granulated sugar
- 4 large eggs
- 2 cups of all-purpose flour
- 1 tsp baking powder
- 1/2 tsp baking soda
- 1/2 tsp ground cinnamon
- 1/4 tsp ground nutmeg
- 1/4 tsp ground cloves
- 1/4 tsp salt
- 1/2 cup of milk (any type)
- 1 tsp vanilla extract

Instructions

1. Set your oven to 300°F (150°C) and turn it on. Grease and line with parchment paper a round 9-inch (23cm) cake pan.

2. Put the mixed dried fruits and chopped nuts in a bowl. Mix them well by tossing them together.
3. In a separate big bowl, beat the melted butter and granulated sugar until they are light and fluffy.
4. Add the eggs one by one, mixing well after everyone.
5. Mix the all-purpose flour, nutmeg, cloves, baking powder, cinnamon, baking soda, and salt with a whisk.
6. Mix the butter and sugar until they are smooth. Then, slowly add the dry ingredients and alternate with the milk. Please start with the dry ingredients and end with them.
7. Add the vanilla extract and mix well.
8. Mix the chopped nuts and dried fruits until they are spread out evenly in the batter.
9. Pour the batter into the cake pan that has already been greased, and use a spatula to smooth the top.
10. Bake in a preheated oven for about 2 hours and 30 minutes, or until a toothpick in the middle of the cake comes out clean.
11. Take the cake out of the oven and let it cool for 10 minutes in the pan. Then, move it to a wire rack to finish cooling.
12. Once the Fruit Cake has cooled, please put it in a container that won't let air in. It can be eaten immediately or put in the fridge for a few days to let the tastes develop.

Nutrition Information (per serving, based on 12 servings)

Calories: 420 Carbohydrates: 54g Protein: 6g Fat: 21g Fiber: 3g

Carrot Cookies

Preparation Time: 20 minutes

Cooking Time: 12-15 minutes

Total Time: 32-35 minutes

Ingredients

- 1 cup of grated carrots
- 1/2 cup of unsalted butter, softened
- 1/2 cup of granulated sugar
- 1/2 cup of brown sugar
- 1 large egg
- 1 tsp vanilla extract
- 1 3/4 cups of all-purpose flour
- 1 tsp baking powder
- 1/2 tsp baking soda
- 1/2 tsp ground cinnamon
- 1/4 tsp ground nutmeg
- 1/4 tsp salt
- 1/2 cup of raisins or chopped nuts (optional)

Instructions

1. Set your oven to 350°F (175°C) and turn it on. Put parchment paper on a baking sheet.
2. Cream the melted butter, white sugar, and brown sugar in a bowl until light and fluffy.
3. To the butter and sugar mixture, add the egg and vanilla extract. Beat until everything is well mixed.
4. Mix the baking powder, all-purpose flour, ground nutmeg, baking soda, ground cinnamon, and salt in a separate bowl.
5. Mix the dry and wet components gradually.
6. Stir in the grated carrots and raisins or chopped nuts, if you're using them until they are spread out evenly in the dough.

7. Place spoonfuls of cookie dough about 2 inches apart on the baking sheet that has been prepared.
8. Bake in an oven that has been warm for 12 to 15 minutes or until the edges turn yellow.
9. Take the cookies out of the oven and let them cool for a few minutes on the baking sheet. Then, move them to a wire rack to cool fully.
10. Store the Carrot Cookies at room temperature in a jar that won't let air in.

Nutrition Information (per serving, based on 1 cookie)

Calories: 120 Carbohydrates: 17g Protein: 1g Fat: 6g Fiber: 1g

Hot Chocolate Pudding

Preparation Time: 15 minutes

Cooking Time: 15 minutes

Total Time: 30 minutes

Ingredients

- 1/2 cup of granulated sugar
- 1/4 cup of unsweetened cocoa powder
- 1/4 cup of cornstarch
- 1/4 tsp salt
- 2 3/4 cups of milk (any type)
- 1/2 cup of semisweet chocolate chips
- 1 tsp vanilla extract
- Whipped cream, marshmallows, or chocolate shavings for topping (optional)

Instructions

1. Whisk the powdered sugar, cocoa powder, cornstarch, and salt in a medium pot until everything is well-mixed.
2. Whisk in the milk slowly, breaking up cocoa powder or cornstarch lumps.
3. Set the pot over medium heat and stir until it thickens and boils. It should take 10–12 minutes to do this.
4. Turn down the heat and stir in the chocolate chips until they melt and the mixture is smooth.
5. Take the pan off the heat and add the vanilla extract while stirring.
6. Pour the hot chocolate pudding into small or big bowls to serve many people.
7. Put plastic wrap or wax paper on the pudding to prevent skin formation.
8. Let the pudding cool to room temperature, and then put it in the fridge for at least two hours to set and cold.
9. Serve the Hot Chocolate Pudding cold, with whipped cream, marshmallows, or chocolate bits on top.

Nutrition Information

Calories: 240 Carbohydrates: 44g Protein: 5g Fat: 7g Fiber: 3g

Roasted Plums with Walnut Crumble

Preparation Time: 15 minutes

Cooking Time: 25 minutes

Total Time: 40 minutes

Ingredients

For the Roasted Plums

- 6 plums, halved and pitted
- 2 tbsp honey or maple syrup
- 1 tbsp lemon juice
- 1/2 tsp ground cinnamon
- 1/4 tsp ground nutmeg

For the Walnut Crumble Topping:

- 1/2 cup of all-purpose flour
- 1/4 cup of rolled oats
- 1/4 cup of chopped walnuts
- 2 tbsp brown sugar
- 2 tbsp unsalted butter, melted

Instructions

1. Preheat your oven to 375°F (190°C). Grease a baking dish.
2. Mix the plums cut in half in a bowl and have the pits taken out, honey or maple syrup, lemon juice, cinnamon powder, and nutmeg powder. Toss the plums gently until they are all covered.
3. Put the plums, cut side up, in the prepared baking dish.
4. Mix together all-purpose flour, rolled oats, chopped walnuts, brown sugar, and melted butter in a separate bowl for the walnut crumble topping. Stir the ingredients together until they are well mixed and crumbly.
5. Spread the crumble topping with walnuts evenly over the plums.
6. Bake in an oven that has already been warm for 20 to 25 minutes or until the plums are soft and the topping is golden brown.
7. Take it out of the oven and wait a few minutes before serving.
8. Serve the Roasted Plums with Walnut Crumble warm, with vanilla ice cream or whipped cream.

Nutrition Information (per serving)

Calories: 220 Carbohydrates: 34g Protein: 3g Fat: 9g Fiber: 4g

Mascarpone and Honey Figs

Preparation Time: 10 minutes

Cooking Time: 5 minutes

Total Time: 15 minutes

Ingredients

- 8 ripe figs
- 1/4 cup of mascarpone cheese
- 2 tbsp honey
- 1/4 cup of chopped walnuts or pistachios (optional)
- Fresh mint leaves for garnish (optional)

Instructions

1. Preheat your oven to 350°F (175°C).
2. Half the figs along their length.
3. Cut side up, put the fig halves on a baking sheet.
4. Pour the honey over the figs and make sure to spread it out evenly.

5. Bake the figs in an oven that has already been hot for about 5 minutes or until they are soft and slightly browned.
6. While the figs are baking, mix the mascarpone cheese in a small bowl until it is smooth.
7. Take the figs out of the oven and give them a few minutes to cool down.
8. Serve the honey-roasted figs with dollops of mascarpone cheese on a plate or dish.
9. If you want more crunch, sprinkle chopped walnuts or peanuts on top, or decorate with fresh mint leaves.
10. Mascarpone and Honey Figs are delicious, while the figs are still hot.

Nutrition Information (per serving, based on 2 fig halves with mascarpone)

Calories: 180 Carbohydrates: 26g Protein: 3g Fat: 9g Fiber: 3g

Pistachio-Stuffed Dates

Preparation Time: 15 minutes

Cooking Time: 0 minutes

Total Time: 15 minutes

Ingredients

- 12 Medjool dates, pitted
- 24 unsalted pistachios (2 per date)
- Optional: drizzle of honey or a sprinkle of sea salt

Instructions

1. Carefully cut every date in half lengthwise to make a hole.
2. Take the dates' pits out.

3. Take two peanuts and carefully place them inside every date.
4. Put some pressure on the dates to close up the space around the nuts.
5. Put the stuffed dates on a plate to serve.
6. Drizzle a little honey over the stuffed dates to add more taste, or sprinkle them with a pinch of sea salt.
7. Serve the dates with pistachios right away as a tasty snack or dessert.

Nutrition Information (per serving, based on 2 stuffed dates)

Calories: 120 Carbohydrates: 27g Protein: 2g Fat: 1g Fiber: 3g

END

Printed in Great Britain
by Amazon

41023668R00064